AMERICAN PLAYWRIGHTS 1945-75

AMERICAN PLAYWRIGHTS 1945-75

Catharine Hughes

Pitman Publishing

First Published 1976

SIR ISAAC PITMAN AND SONS LTD
Pitman House, Parker Street, Kingsway, London WC2B 5PB
PO Box 46038, Banda Street, Nairobi, Kenya

PITMAN PUBLISHING PTY LTD
Pitman House, 158 Bouverie Street, Carlton, Victoria 3053, Australia

PITMAN PUBLISHING CORPORATION
6 East 43 Street, New York, NY 10017, USA

SIR ISAAC PITMAN (CANADA) LTD
495 Wellington Street West, Toronto 135, Canada

THE COPP CLARK PUBLISHING COMPANY
517 Wellington Street West, Toronto 135, Canada

© Catharine Hughes 1976

Portions of several chapters have appeared in different form in *America, The
Critic* and *Plays and Players*.

Cased edition ISBN: 0273 00752 1
Paperback edition ISBN: 0 273 00756 4

Text set in 11/12 pt. Photon Baskerville, printed by photolithography,
and bound in Great Britain at The Pitman Press, Bath

G. 3548/3552 : 15

Contents

If you wish to be a playwright
you just leave the theatre of tomorrow
to take care of itself.

Noël Coward

What matters is whether it's a
good show or not.

Laurence Olivier

1 Introduction

In the years immediately following World War II, American playwriting seemed on the brink of its first golden age. First, though originally rather tentatively, came Arthur Miller with a failure, *The Man Who Had All the Luck,* in 1944, followed by the award-winning *All My Sons* and *Death of a Salesman,* which remains one of the most striking and impressive American dramas since O'Neill. Tennessee Williams' *The Glass Menagerie* was staged in 1945 and quickly followed by *A Streetcar Named Desire* in 1947, then *Cat on a Hot Tin Roof,* each in its way a powerful and arresting work. In 1950, William Inge came on the scene with *Come Back, Little Sheba,* shortly following with *Picnic* in 1953 and *Bus Stop* in 1955. All were young men — an average age of thirty-four — when they achieved their first Broadway production.

And the possibilities were in no sense exhausted by this apparently powerful triumverate. Robert Anderson, whose *Come Marching Home,* the story of a returning war veteran who enters politics, had been produced by the Off Broadway Blackfriars Guild in 1945, attracted major attention and a long run with the then controversial *Tea and Sympathy*, in which a boy is accused of homosexuality, in 1953. Arthur Laurents weighed in with the interesting, if less successful, *Home of the Brave* in 1945, *The Time of the Cuckoo* (1952) and *A Clearing in the Woods* (1952), among others, and Paddy Chayefsky with such plays as *Middle of the Night* and *The Tenth Man*. Several highly successful television playwrights—Horton Foote, Tad Mosel, N. Richard Nash, Robert Alan Aurthur and David Shaw, together with Chayefsky—formed an organization similar to the Playwrights' Company to produce their theatrical works. Gore Vidal was writing plays; so were Rod Serling, William Gibson (most notably, *The Miracle Worker*) and Ira Levin (*No Time for Sergeants*). In addition, various playwrights who had established reputations prior to World War II continued to be at least sporadically active, among them Lillian Hellman, S. N. Behrman, Elmer Rice (though he had his last Broadway success with *Dream Girl*, in 1945), Maxwell Anderson, Robert E. Sherwood, Thornton Wilder, Clifford Odets and Sidney Kingsley. None were, in fact, major playwrights, though each had his moment or moments in the theatrical sun, some of them well-deserved.

Towering over all, of course, was the resurgence of Eugene O'Neill, which began with the Off Broadway revival of *The Iceman Cometh* in 1956 and took on the proportions of a boom with the Broadway production of *Long Day's Journey into Night* later that year. Although O'Neill, who was born on 16 October, 1888, and died in 1953, cannot truly be termed a 'postwar' playwright, despite the fact that some of his most significant works have been produced since 1945, it would be almost impossible to discuss American playwriting since World War II without at least briefly discussing him.

Some years ago, when the American quarterly *Modern Drama* devoted an issue to O'Neill, one of the contributors observed that 'O'Neill's trajectory presents the only accomplished life of any playwright in our country'.

Whether O'Neill was a great playwright may be open to conjecture; his catalytic role in the history of the American theatre is not. At a time when American dramatists were scarcely recognized either in their own nation or abroad he appeared on the scene with all the light, the fire, the agony and the aspiration of a nation coming of age. A man of the theatre—his father was the actor James O'Neill of *Monte Cristo* fame—he nonetheless managed to separate himself from it sufficiently to achieve the distinction of being a writer first, a theatrical subject second. It is not as easy as it sounds.

O'Neill's absorption in every detail of production, particularly in his early years at the Provincetown Theatre, is almost legendary. Yet, unlike playwrights who have been so much its willing victim, he succeeded in avoiding the captivity of the hothouse, inbred existence that is Broadway. O'Neill thus became that unique combination: a writer at once completely at home in the theatre, one fully aware of its potentialities, but one who, when the moment periodically arrived, could recognize its trap. A dramatist of extraordinary power and theatricality, he was a man of extreme insecurity and reticence. In complement to each other, these qualities evolved the one American dramatist who, when he failed—as he often did—did so with something approaching the grandeur of querulous and searching genius, and who, when he succeeded, did it with a magnitude transcending much of the petty cavilling of even the most academic of critics.

Any attempt to assess O'Neill's stature as a dramatist is open to more than the usual number of pitfalls. To an extent greater than that of almost any other modern playwright, his work offered an almost continual oscillation between the exceptional and the mediocre. As a consequence, the O'Neill canon and myth are mined with frustration and disappointment more often than with gold. It is perhaps this more than any other factor which accounts for the alternating periods of worship and deflation to which he has been subjected.

To a very considerable extent, O'Neill can be said to have been both the benefactor and the victim of his myth. And, in both cases, he was its not altogether unwilling abettor. It is probable, however, that European assessments of O'Neill have been more realistic than those of American critics who, all too often, have felt called upon to be either chauvinistically laudatory or consciously debunking.

European criticism of O'Neill is revealing for two distinct, though not unrelated reasons. The first and most important is the understanding it reflects of what O'Neill was: of his dramatic antecedents, his innovations and what he was striving to do. The second is its relative consistency—at least by comparison with his fluctuating American reputation. A 1946 survey by George Jean Nathan in the *American Mercury* found O'Neill's critical reception in France, Italy, Greece, Australia, the Soviet Union, Romania, the Scandinavian countries—and China—'extremely favourable', and that in Germany almost comparably so. In the Soviet Union, Tairov's world-famous Kamerny Theatre enjoyed perhaps its greatest post-Revolution success with O'Neill's works. In such plays as *The Hairy Ape*, *All God's Chillun Got Wings* and *Desire Under the Elms*, Tairov found themes exploring labour and race problems which, though they were not written from a Marxist viewpoint, were sufficiently close to the approach dictated by the Soviet government. It was a time when O'Neill was in considerable critical disrepute in his homeland.

Volumes could be—indeed, have been—compiled on O'Neill criticism alone. Since he is virtually the lone

American playwright thus far accorded this distinction, it is perhaps as good an indication as one is likely to find of his significance in American and world theatre. Numerous lamentations concerning O'Neill's lack of discipline, his frequently bombastic language, his too obvious symbolism, the dialogue that one reviewer termed 'a string of clichés', all somehow pale in the face of those occasional moments when, by whatever means, grandness of conception and the capacity to strive for what may very well be unattainable mesh with that peculiar quality only realized in the infrequent meeting of an artist, his art and his audience.

The ups and downs of the O'Neill career have been widely recounted. From early frustration to early Off Broadway adulation; from vast commercial and critical success to their opposites, O'Neill ran the gamut. On a critical level, it sometimes seemed that his popularity in itself was the only necessary testimony to his artistic inferiority. Or, as Mary McCarthy once observed on seeing a play both she *and* the public had liked: 'Could this mean there was something the matter with me? Was I starting to sell out?' The fact that O'Neill could both probe deeply and be almost outrageously superficial; that he could achieve the heights of a *Long Day's Journey into Night* and the turgid inadequacies of *A Touch of the Poet*—and occasionally worse—is in itself one of the great dichotomies of dramatic literature. The language: soaring and poetic at one moment, pedestrian and plodding the next; the characters: here brilliantly conceived, there caricatures and clichés; all these factors crossed and criss-crossed in O'Neill's concept of a theatre that was life—'the substance and interpretation of life'—a life in which 'we are always seeing further than we can reach'.

As a writer, O'Neill frequently drew upon his own obsessions. In itself, of course, this is far from unique. O'Neill, however, by chance or otherwise, used them in such a way as to give birth to the two plays which almost undoubtedly are his greatest: *The Iceman Cometh* and *Long Day's Journey*.

Iceman, written in 1939, did not have its American premiere until September of 1946, when, in an at least partially ineffective production, it enjoyed something less than the substantial success it was to have in an extraordinary Off Broadway revival ten years later. In a sense, *Iceman* represented a personal summation for O'Neill, just as *Long Day's Journey* was an attempt to reconcile and to purge the family ghosts of his 'curse of the misbegotten'. It was, he told an interviewer, 'a play about pipe dreams. And the philosophy is that there is always one dream left, one final dream, no matter how low you have fallen, down there at the bottom of the bottle. I know because I saw it'.

More than 'pipe dreams', more than illusions, the thing O'Neill came to grips with in *Iceman* was his near lifelong obsession with death, that death which was the only escape from the pipe dreams, the fears, which prove that 'the best of all were never to be born'. In Harry Hope's saloon men feed on cheap liquor and live off their illusions. Temporarily deprived of them by the crusading Hickey, they find life a void, a meaningless and intolerable passing of hours and days, days they know will be filled only by their failure. It is not enough. Grasping for straws, they find them; they return to that world of illusion in which all things are possible and tomorrow is always *tomorrow*. But for Hickey with his Iceman Death; for young Parritt, who carries a guilt he cannot shift; and most of all for the philosophical Larry, their pipe dreams destroyed beyond reclaiming, death, or the hope of it, is the only way out.

Its philosophical transparency can be laid aside. *Iceman* is an extremely moving and powerful work. Like nearly all that the later O'Neill wrote, it is verbose and would without doubt have benefited from cutting. Yet, when that has been said, it remains, with *Long Day's Journey*, a towering theatrical achievement. Its depth of conviction, the life from which it sprang, its sheer intensity, make it impossible to escape or ignore. It displays a willingness, indeed an eagerness, to pose what O'Neill once contended was his only concern, 'the relation between man and God'. If O'Neill's 'answers' are frequently unsatisfactory, one can perhaps only suggest that it is not the artist's role to *answer* while at the same time acknowledging O'Neill's ability to make the questions more than merely symbolic and their dramatization an experience rather than an experiment.

Most of the criticism that has been levelled against *Iceman* is equally appropriate to *Long Day's Journey*. The same is true of the praise. The importance of the play, however, extends considerably beyond its intrinsic merits, substantial though they are. It is both the play most responsible for the reappraisal of O'Neill after his long period of relative neglect and, as Harold Clurman has noted, 'the testament of the most serious playwright our country has produced'.

Because it probes deeply the sources of its author's second demon—his family heritage—*Long Day's Journey* is a drama abounding in guilt and attempts at understanding. It is, nearly alone among his works, a play in which the dialógue reveals a genuine poetry in contrast to O'Neill's generally more pedestrian language.

Long Day's Journey is almost pure auto-biography—from the penurious actor-father to the drug-addicted mother; the alcoholic older brother to the tubercular younger (O'Neill himself). In young Edmund, O'Neill experiences his attempt at explanation and expiation, his ultimate inability to grasp his family's 'fate'. It remains, however, for Mary Tyrone to express the idea that had plagued O'Neill almost from his coming to a consciousness of what 'life' was: 'None of us can help the things life has done to us. They're done before you realize it, and once they're done they make you do other things until at last everything comes between you and what you'd like to be, and you've lost your true self forever.'

O'Neill's groping to find that lost self was apparent, in one form or another, in nearly all his plays. This is especially true in *Days Without End*, a relatively ineffectual drama, but one interesting because of its origin: O'Neill's lost, lamented Roman Catholicism. A Catholic in his childhood, he early left the Church and throughout his life betrayed an unconcealed nostalgia for it. In *Days Without End*, as elsewhere, he was unsuccessful in portraying his abandoned faith; the sense of loss was something else entirely. By most accounts, it continued to occupy O'Neill in later years, although he, unlike the John Loving of the play, was never to return.

While O'Neill frequently aspired far beyond his final accomplishment, his vision of the theatre's possibilities was, in a very real sense, his greatest achievement. The number of areas he opened to the American dramatist—or, in some instances, re-established—is extraordinary. From naturalism and melodrama to expressionism; plays involving masks; the use of the aside; the depiction of split personality; the employment of such things as drum beats and engine rhythms as an integral aspect of drama; the development of a new level of philosophical and psychological awareness in theatre—the list could be considerably extended. At a time when the American theatre could ill afford to look at itself in a mirror, it was primarily O'Neill who raised it to the level where its purpose, if not necessarily its attainments, again became in accord with its possibilities.

Tennessee Williams has observed that O'Neill 'gave birth to the American theatre and died for it'. While the statement betrays Williams' penchant for melodrama, it also contains a strong element of truth, at least in its initial aspect. O'Neill's influence on the American writers who followed him in the postwar years is virtually incalculable. Williams himself, of course, William Inge, Edward Albee and others to one extent or another display their debt to him. More than this, however, O'Neill lent stature to the American dramatist as such, removing him from the limbo of theatrical forgotten men to which lack of talent and early twentieth-century Broadway managements had consigned him. The Swiss dramatist Friedrich Duerrenmatt has suggested that O'Neill 'will continue to grow'. A certain few of his plays surely will; and, if there was any reason to think postwar American drama was on the brink of the aforementioned golden age, he unquestionably deserves a great deal of the credit for it.

Regrettably, however, that golden age did not materialize, even though it seemed about to have a second generation when Edward Albee came on the scene with *The Zoo Story* and *Who's Afraid of Virginia Woolf?*, Jack Gelber with *The Connection* (1959) and Jack Richardson with *The Prodigal* (1960).

The question inevitably arises: What happened? After all the initial promise, all the initial successes, what happened to all these writers who, at least at the time, seemed to possess the potential to become major dramatists? Williams, Miller and Albee in a sense have, at least in the generally accepted meaning of the term. More accurately, however, a play or two—in Williams' case, three—have given them a certain stature. Regardless of more recent works, each of their new plays is an eagerly anticipated theatrical 'event', a source of hope that their earliest plays will be matched or bettered. Realistically, the bright possibilities and even brighter expectations have been almost entirely defaulted upon, with the field left to Neil Simon, who today makes a for the most part ineffectual effort to be taken 'seriously' by the critics if not the public.

In the years since 1945, the 'serious' American

playwright has in general been a man without a home, at least a man without a theatre. (For reasons I will get to shortly, what might be termed the 'third generation' of postwar playwrights may be faring considerably better.) In the period before World War II—despite the Depression—he could look to Broadway. Indeed, he could still look there in the years immediately following the war. In the past two decades, however, that situation has altered beyond recognition. Williams, certainly the most important of the postwar American playwrights, has had to resort to Off Broadway for the production of two of his last three plays; the third, *Out Cry*, closed after a handful of performances and his most recent, *The Red Devil Battery Sign* (1975), closed in Boston after two weeks of try-out performances in mid-1975. Whatever one may think of Arthur Miller's most recent work, *The Creation of the World and Other Business*—and I am among the majority who thought very little of it—Miller's position in the American theatre alone theoretically should have insured him a more than twenty-performance hearing. That Albee's work continues, albeit unsuccessfully, to be produced on Broadway owes at least as much to his partnership in the sponsoring production company as to any appreciable Broadway audience interest.

For a decade or more, Off Broadway seemed the obvious solution, at least for the younger writer not already imbued with the Broadway mystique. The situation was short-lived. By late 1975, there were not only far fewer productions on view, but, on a random day, the five commercially sponsored plays numbered three musicals or revues, one sexploitation musical and *one* original play, which had been running for well over two years.

The condition in 1975 did not reflect a sudden turn of events. Gradually, as the economics of Off Broadway had narrowed the possibilities of a producer recouping his investment in a straight play, theatres had gone dark and often remained that way throughout an entire season or seasons. As on Broadway, where musicals have been known to run for over two years and still experience a substantial loss, money was to be made only with the hit, either the musical or the sex or gay exploitation show, where, to say the least, the playwright is a minimal contributor.

Obviously, things have reached a sorry pass for the playwright—other than Simon—who continues to retain the illusion that a life in the American commercial theatre is possible. An occasional freak hit, such as Lanford Wilson's *The Hot L Baltimore*, first produced off-Off Broadway, is simply the exception that proves the rule.

In the sixties, then, one—whether playwright or so-called serious theatregoer—increasingly began to look to off-Off Broadway, where the quality of the shoe-string productions often did not match the quality of the plays (especially in the early days), but where production, discovery and excitement at least seemed—and were—possible. There was from the first, however, largely a coterie audience for off-Off Broadway. Playwrights, directors, actors, even critics (which, in retrospect, was to prove the most unfortunate of all), provided a large part of each other's audiences. There were, and have continued to be, exceptions, but, in general, there evolved an in-bred atmosphere in which, all too often, the plays written and presented were written and presented with this elite in mind. (I should, perhaps, note that neither as critic nor as playwright do I plead any innocence in this, having done my own share in perpetuating it.)

Two things happened. On the one hand, many of the plays and the productions became increasingly self-indulgent. On the other, when critics from what can only be termed the 'outside' began to review productions—admittedly, some of them only out of desperation over the commercial theatre—what had occurred Off Broadway began, so far on a much more limited scale, to happen off-Off Broadway. It, or at least part of it, began to seek out potential 'hits', plays or musicals that would 'try-out' off-Off Broadway and, after a rave review in the *New York Times* or occasionally elsewhere, move to commercial production, sometimes with the cast intact, sometimes with more professional, or more box-office, casts and, more rarely, directors.

Clearly, none of this was good for the vast majority of the off-Off Broadway playwrights. Although the jury is still out, as it should be, since most of the playwrights are only in their thirties or early forties, the signs at the moment are not especially auspicious.

In the end, in the theatre, though not necessarily in music, the dance and the novel, popularity—or, more accurately, public recognition and acceptance—has been at least one criterion in estimating a writer's stature. A poet may write a play of lyrical virtuosity, a philosopher or a metaphysician one possessing profound and brilliant insights. Yet, if his work does not come alive in the theatre, come alive, that is, for an audience beyond a limited number of colleagues and sympathizers, it is not really a successful play, not a successful play at all. The Webster dictionary, in one of its definitions, describes theatre as 'dramatic effectiveness'.

Lest this seem a brief for 'popular', commercial, hit-oriented theatre, it is worth noting that the major playwrights of the past—whether the Greeks, Shakespeare, Molière or Shaw, to name but a few—or the present—Beckett, Brecht, Pinter, Williams—have not written for either the closet or the desk drawer. They have written, occasionally abstrusely, occasionally didactically, in an effort to entertain, communicate with, inform, convert, even educate, an audience far beyond their own circle. One of the problems of off-Off Broadway has been a direct outgrowth of one of its virtues: where there is no necessity, either economic or social, to achieve a wider audience, it becomes too easy a matter—especially on a series of Foundation grants—not to do so.

All of this, of course, sounds frightfully reactionary, and, needless to say, one could point to a small number of playwrights who have come out of the basements and lofts to achieve somewhat wider audiences. Lanford Wilson is one of them, Terrence McNally and, to a lesser extent, Israel Horovitz and Paul Foster, others. Tom Eyen had a great commercial success with *The Dirtiest Show in Town*, but, with all due lack of respect, *The Dirtiest Show* is hardly what off-Off Broadway has purported to be about. LeRoi Jones and Ed Bullins, the best of the black playwrights—and among the best playwrights of whatever race of their generation—are less a product of off-Off Broadway than of the emerging black theatrical consciousness and belatedly growing black theatre audience. As a force, off-Off Broadway has little right to claim them. Many of the other more prominent and widely heralded of the early off-Off Broadway playwrights have been either relatively or completely silent in recent years or turned to other forms. Off-Off Broadway itself has increasingly resorted, though not yet predominantly, to revivals, with several groups now devoted more or less entirely to them.

There has, fortunately, been what is still, in America, a very new force which has come to the rescue: the so-called institutional theatre, which in New York means primarily the New York Shakespeare Festival, operating out of five theatres in its Public Theatre building and two at the Lincoln Center for the Performing Arts, the Chelsea Theatre Center of Brooklyn, with one theatre in that borough and another in Manhattan, and the American Place Theatre, which operates on an exclusively subscription basis, producing both new plays and revivals.

Without question, they have offered the new hope of the American playwright and the American theatre. David Rabe, Jason Miller, Robert Montgomery, Charles Gordone and, more recently, Michael Weller, are Public Theatre playwrights. The Chelsea Theatre Center, dividing its schedule between new plays and carefully thought out revivals, has brought to its audiences some of the most exhilarating theatre of the period. The American Place, despite some exceedingly bad play selection in recent seasons, remains a haven for the playwright and provides some of the most highly professional productions to be found in New York. The newer Circle Repertory Theatre has given revitalized creative impetus to Lanford Wilson and others and a first theatrical life to several playwrights who hold out substantial promise for the future.

If one were inclined, one could, I daresay, point with opprobrium to the fact that virtually without exception these members of the younger generation of American playwrights are now, regardless of their stylistic predilections, writing to communicate and not self-consciously to obscure and that those who continue to do the latter have failed to move on in terms either of craft or of acceptance.

At the height of the off-Off Broadway movement, there were over a hundred theatres and there are only marginally fewer today. With such volume, one inevitably has to speculate on just how much of genuine or enduring significance they have produced over some fifteen years. Despite some highlights, the answer is, regrettably, relatively little. Although an argument could be made for the point that a *single* work of genuinely inspired genius would be sufficient to justify the movement, it would be simply a debater's point. Off-Off Broadway *has* produced any number of exceptionally worthwhile, exceptionally entertaining plays. It has nurtured some writers who in the future may develop to the point of being considered major, Shepard, Wilson and Van Itallie being the most obvious among them. It has not, however, lived up to either its reputation or the expectations it generated and its work over the past few years has, if anything, shown less indication that it will.

Although some of the playwrights of the immediate postwar generation have continued to write for the theatre, the results have been disappointing. Robert Anderson, who for a brief time was grouped by some critics with 'Williams–Miller–Inge' (which became almost generic), followed *Tea and Sympathy* with *All Summer Long* (1954), *Silent Night, Lonely Night* (1959), the highly popular *You Know I Can't Hear You When the Water's Running* (four one-acts produced in 1967) and the considerably less successful *I Never Sang for My Father* (1968), *The Days Between* (1970) and *Solitaire/Double Solitaire* (1971), none of which have given any indication that Anderson, now nearing sixty, belongs in the front rank to which he was once being all too prematurely consigned.

Arthur Laurents has taken primarily to writing the books for musicals, most notably *West Side Story* and *Gypsy*, though he did author the ineffectual 1973 Off Broadway play *The Enclave*. In the autumn of 1959, Louis Kronenberger wrote in the *Partisan Review* that 'amid the honest intentions of Arthur Laurents's *A Clearing in the Woods*, which is most depressing?—his attempting a kind of crude stream-of-consciousness so late in the day; or in so wrong and distant a medium; or with such uneven and limited gifts'. With *The Enclave*, the stream-of-consciousness had fortunately disappeared, but the unevenness and limited gifts were all too obviously in evidence. He has recently completed a new play, *Scream*.

After the failure of *The Latent Heterosexual* (Dallas, 1967; Royal Shakespeare Company, 1968), which did not come to New York, Paddy Chayefsky apparently abandoned the theatre for films. In 1969, he wrote that 'Broadway as a legitimate theatre is moribund'. By 1975, the fifty-two-year-old playwright had not changed his mind. 'In the foreseeable future, I see nothing for me on Broadway', he told an interviewer. 'It's really because there are no audiences. The theatre has become a kind of unnecessary institution.'

This, perhaps, reflects the prevailing attitude of many if not most of the better-known, theoretically 'serious' American playwrights of Chayefsky's generation, who, occasional forays aside, have deserted the theatre in favour of films, television, the novel or the memoir. With most, at least on the basis of prior performance, the loss cannot be said to have been a major one, in some cases because essentially they were merely dabbling in the theatre, in most because theirs were and are minor talents.

None of this, however, does anything to mitigate the highly unfavourable circumstances under which both they and those who have elected to remain active in the theatre have almost invariably had to operate. This holds true whether it be Inge agonizing over what he, with some justification, considered the Broadway theatre's destruction and the subsequent quick demise of *A Loss of Roses* in 1959, or a younger playwright experiencing the anger and frustration that inevitably arise when a new play, whether on Broadway or off, closes within a week despite respectful, and sometimes enthusiastic notices.

If the circumstances are poor, the auguries, apart from the possibilities offered by the previously mentioned theatre companies, would if anything seem to be even worse for the playwright with anything approaching serious intentions to reach an other than very limited audience, as even Neil Simon has recently begun to discover. It would be pleasant, at least for a critic, to be able to lay all the blame at the door of the audience, pleasant but inaccurate. There must, after all, have been a reason why the disenchantment set in in the first place, since dance, to name but one of the other performing arts, has been enjoying a period of phenomenal growth both qualitatively and quantitatively at precisely the same time and concert halls, art galleries and museums a more modest but still impressive increase in attendance. Heretical though it may seem, perhaps it is time that those who blame the audiences, or the critics, or the unions, look to something else—the product.

That said, it seems advisable to raise a question. Although the pages that follow may seem excessively hard on most of the playwrights under consideration, what discussion of a particular country's playwrights over the past three decades could in honesty go much easier? Williams, Miller, Inge, Albee and company have each produced at least two or three plays that rank among the major dramatic works of the period. Can one say much more of Fry and Rattigan and Osborne, or of Ionesco and Anouilh, Grass, Hochhuth and Weiss? Perhaps one can of Pinter, and his development would seem to indicate that the best is yet ahead, which cannot be said for the quartet of Americans named above.

Samuel Beckett is, of course, a case apart, though any national claims on him—whether 'French', 'Irish' or simply English-speaking—are highly suspect.

In saying this, I am making no attempt to score points for the American playwrights of the post-World War II period. As anyone who reads the following pages will find quite evident, I see relatively little of comfort in the American theatre as it enters the final quarter of the twentieth century. There does, however, exist potential, even considerable potential, the nature of which will be discussed in some of the individual chapters and particularly in the conclusion.

2 Tennessee Williams

Although one hears an occasional claim for Arthur Miller, Tennessee Williams is by general consensus the most significant American playwright to emerge during the period that began roughly at the end of World War II. Even while agreeing with the consensus, one has to find it a bit surprising, not to say disconcerting. It has been nearly fifteen years since Williams' last major critical success, *The Night of the Iguana*, won the New York Drama Critics Circle Award in 1961. In more recent years, such theoretically major works as *Kingdom of Earth* and *Out Cry* have been deserved critical and box office failures, while *In the Bar of a Tokyo Hotel* and *Small Craft Warnings*, both produced Off Broadway, have fallen far short of the early plays that established Williams' reputation; as has *The Red Devil Battery Sign* (1975). It hardly lessens the conundrum to note that his first Broadway play and first success, *The Glass Menagerie*, remains his best play. It was produced in 1945.

Williams' career has, as it happens, followed a pattern similar to that of many, perhaps most, of the American dramatists and novelists of the past three decades: the initial great success and great expectations, the subsequent critical and public disenchantment, the repeated suggestion over the past decade that he is 'written out', though *Menagerie*, *A Streetcar Named Desire* and perhaps *Cat on a Hot Tin Roof* cannot themselves be written off. It remains for the social scientists to explore Scott Fitzgerald's contention that there are no 'second acts' in American life, at least in the life of the American artist. America's writers frequently tend to confirm it.

Yet Williams' career remains in many ways a remarkable one both in terms of its highlights and its productivity. Born Thomas Lanier Williams (he adopted the 'Tennessee' years later) in Columbus, Mississippi, on 26 March, 1911, he graduated from the University of Iowa in 1938. (Among other things, he had, like the narrator of *The Glass Menagerie*, worked for a shoe company, which Tom Wingfield in that play calls a 'living death', in between.) He first achieved limited national recognition with an award from the Group Theatre in 1939, and his first major production came with *Battle of Angels*, which closed in Boston during a pre-Broadway try-out run in 1940. (It was subsequently rewritten as *Orpheus Descending*, 1957.)

It was, however, with *The Glass Menagerie*, which one critic, with some exaggeration but considerable validity, has asserted was 'the beginning of a new epoch in Western theatre history', that Williams was established as a significant figure in the postwar American theatre. Not surprisingly, it displayed many of the themes and preoccupations that were to absorb him over the next thirty years. In a preface to the published version, Williams refers to it as initiating 'a new, plastic theatre which must take the place of the exhausted theatre of realistic conventions if the theatre is to resume vitality as part of our culture'.

Whether it was that is dubious; that it was the first significant and enduring 'postwar' American play is beyond challenge.

The Glass Menagerie is set in the thirties, when America was in the throes of the Depression and labour disturbances were to be found in many, perhaps most, cities. Williams' narrator, Tom Wingfield, calls it 'a memory play . . . sentimental . . . not realistic', and this surely is true, in its way, but the saga of Tom, Laura and Amanda Wingfield *is* in many ways realistic, with Tom, who displays so many characteristics of Williams himself—poet, free spirit, one of the playwright's 'fugitive kind'. Like Williams, as noted earlier, Tom is an employee in a shoe factory. Amanda, Tom's mother, deserted by her husband, surely has her genesis in the playwright's own mother, one of the once gracious ladies of the now impoverished South, and it is not improbable to suggest that his sister Laura, shy, sensitive, insecure, coming to life almost entirely in terms of her 'glass menagerie' (a collection of glass animals), was inspired by Williams' sister Rose, whose withdrawal from everyday life culminated in a lifelong institutionalization.

It is Laura, victim of a minor physical disability, victim, also, of the world's expectations and demands, who provides the play's focus. She is 'terribly shy', has dropped out of business college after only a few days, a fact unknown to her mother, who fears the twenty-three-year-old girl will become an old maid. She 'lives in a world of her own'. Amanda becomes obsessed with the idea of getting her a 'gentleman caller'. It is an idea that begins to take possession of the Wingfields' apartment and it comes to a form of fruition when Tom, trapped and frustrated in his job at the Continental Shoemakers' warehouse, brings home a more ambitious fellow worker, Jim, 'an emissary from a world of reality that we were somehow set apart from'. For Amanda has suggested to Tom one of Williams' recurring themes, the inroads of time: 'You are the only young man that I know of who ignores the fact that the future becomes the present, the present the past and the past turns into everlasting regret if you don't plan for it!'

Jim's appearance transforms Laura. They had been high school classmates and she had fallen in love with him, though he seems oblivious to her existence. She reveals 'a fragile, unearthly prettiness . . . like a piece of translucent glass touched by light, given a momentary radiance, not actual, not lasting'. Her eager mother, on the other hand, seeking to recover and impress with a 'girlish Southern vivacity', is to Tom only an embarrassment.

Everyone in *The Glass Menagerie* is living a memory or a dream: Amanda with her recollection—or illusion—of how much 'she ought to be loved', Jim O'Connor, with his high school glories, yearbook predictions of success and future expectations, Laura in her isolation, Tom, eager to escape, to join the merchant marine, to write poetry, attempting 'to find in motion what was lost in space'. Even for him, complete escape clearly is not possible: memory makes its demands.

Eventually, Laura and Jim are alone in the Wingfield living room. For Laura it is 'the climax of her secret life', it offers her moment of greatest hope and expectation. For Tom *is* a 'nice, ordinary, young man'—a fact that in itself places him outside the world of Tennessee Williams' principal characters. He correctly diagnoses her feeling of inferiority and she gradually begins to come out of herself. But, after he kisses her, he reveals: 'I've—got strings on me.' He is going to be married on the second Sunday in June.

On Tom's recollection, 'I tried to leave you behind me, but I am more faithful than I intended to be! . . . I buy a drink, I speak to the nearest stranger—anything that can blow your candles out! ... Blow out your candles, Laura—and so good-bye....' she finally does blow them out, as the play ends.

Say what one will about its maudlin moments and its sentimentality, *The Glass Menagerie* is a work of poignance and poetry. Its characters—at least Tom and Laura—have the sensitivity that Williams, too often mistakenly, equates with the poetic or artistic. They are 'different', and 'difference', abnormality, would seem for Williams to be the hallmark of the potential hero or saint, normality its antithesis.

This is equally so in Williams's second major, and second most effective play, *A Streetcar Named Desire* (1947), which received both the New York Drama Critics Circle Award and the Pulitzer Prize, the two most prestigious awards in the American theatre.

Blanche DuBois is another of Williams' fugitive kind. On her first appearance at the Kowalski apartment in New Orleans, she looks as if she were 'arriving at a summer tea or a cocktail party in the garden district'. Daintily dressed in fluffy white, complete to white gloves and hat, she is a being apart. Her appearance, according to the stage directions, 'suggests a moth'.

But this moth can sting—and be stung.

Blanche has come to stay with her younger sister, Stella, and her Polish-American husband, Stanley, in their two-room apartment in a poor section of New Orleans. She is delicate and charming—in her way—but also neurasthenic, sexually hungry. In addition, she is feeling guilty concerning her young husband's suicide. As the days and months pass, it becomes increasingly obvious that she is mentally disturbed, close to desperation. Soon after her arrival, she tells Stella: 'I want to be *near* you, got to be *with* somebody, I *can't* be *alone!* Because—as you must have noticed—I'm *not* very *well.* ...'

Her way of life is gone. Belle Reve, the home of their early days, the myth of another world she clings to, is 'lost'. Her husband, 'a boy, just a boy', had been 'different', possessed 'a nervousness, a softness and tenderness which wasn't like a man's, although he wasn't the least bit effeminate looking'. Then she discovered his homosexuality, 'in the worst of all possible ways'. She had come into a room suddenly, a room she thought was empty. But it was not. Instead, she found 'the boy I had married and an older man who had been his friend for years'. Afterwards, they pretended she knew nothing, but it did not work. Young Allan stuck a revolver in his mouth and shot himself. And Blanche will forever feel guilty, for on the dance floor only moments before she had suddenly, uncontrollably, burst out: 'I saw! I know! You disgust me.'

One of Williams' long line of failed Southern belles, Blanche continually provokes the vulgar, brutish Stanley and gropes toward some kind of relationship with his friend Mitch, only to see that destroyed when Stanley tells him of her reputation for promiscuity in her hometown of Laurel. It seems Blanche had been teaching in the local high school and, 'They kicked her out of that high school before the spring term ended. . . . A seventeen-year-old boy—she'd gotten mixed up with!'

It is, however, the combination of the sexual attraction between Blanche and Stanley and their hatred of each other that provides the heart of the play. Although she attempts to convince Stella she should leave him and insists to her that what he has to offer is 'animal force' and 'the only way to live with such a man is to—go to bed with him! And that's your job—not mine!' the chemistry between them is obvious from the first. When Stella insists there is something deeper between them, Blanche disagrees: 'What you are talking about is brutal desire—just—Desire!—the name of that rattle-trap street-car that bangs through the Quarter.' That desire is, of course, something they share.

While Stella is in the hospital having her baby, Stanley rapes Blanche, after already having bought her a bus ticket to get her out of town. He has just returned home and she tells him she has had a telegram from a Texas oil millionaire inviting her on a cruise of the Caribbean. But it is obviously untrue and the half-drunk Blanche, who has been attempting to pack, is bordering on hysteria. They argue and she goes after him with a broken bottle. It is unreal, a playing out of a scene ordained the moment they met. 'We've had this date with each other from the beginning!' Stanley shouts before carrying her off to bed.

Although Blanche tells Stella, who refuses to believe her, all that remains is her final breakdown and the arrival of the people from a state mental institution, one of whom she tells, in one of the most famous of all Williams' lines: 'I have always depended on the kindness of strangers.'

Williams has said that *Streetcar*'s meaning is 'the ravishment of the tender, the sensitive, the delicate, by the savage and brutal forces of modern society', and that is surely one interpretation that can be placed upon it. It is, however, an oversimplification that denies Blanche's complexity: for she has *her* cruel aspect, her mendacity, to go hand in hand with her fragile vulnerability. Her role in the Kowalski household is threatening and destructive and it is only the fact that Stella and Stanley genuinely do love each other despite their disparate backgrounds and personalities that enables their marriage to endure her presence.

Yet, Blanche is almost the Tennessee Williams archetype. She tells Mitch: 'I don't want realism. I want magic! . . . I don't tell truth, I tell what *ought* to be truth', a line that could be spoken by at least one character in virtually every Williams' play. In writing of the wounded, the fugitive and the mutilated, the solitary, the misfits and the lonely, he suggests a world at once recognizable and apart. Caring deeply—at times perhaps too deeply, if that is possible—about his characters, he writes of them with a compassion that at times borders upon the maudlin. With Blanche, however, the artist's hand is in far firmer control and her characterization and the play as a whole is far more dramatically affecting than is the case in most of the works that have followed.

The Rose Tattoo (1951) and *Camino Real* (1953), for instance, are both far looser in construction and lacking in the narrative focus and intensity of the earlier plays, weighted down by a heavy-handed symbolism not justified in other aspects of the writing. (In *Menagerie*, Williams has Tom say, 'I have a poet's weakness for symbols.' As does his creator—not to mention a penchant for explaining them.)

The Rose Tattoo is set in Serafina's cottage in 'a village populated mostly by Sicilians somewhere along the Gulf Coast between New Orleans and Mobile'. Serafina is Williams' version of an Earth Mother (the role was written for Anna Magnani). Deeply, passionately in love with her husband Rosario, she glories in sex and sexuality. Although a statue of the Madonna stands in a shrine, the bed is Serafina's real altar, the place where she envisions, and has achieved, fulfillment. She also does sewing, as a sign outside proclaims. She recalls waking up in the night and seeing the image of her husband's rose tattoo on her breast and experiencing the certainty that she had conceived, that she is carrying Rosario's second child.

But it is not to be. Rosario drives a truck and under the bananas he hauls is another, illegal, cargo. It is his last trip for the Brothers Romano. After it, he plans to pay for the truck and work for himself, but on that last night he is shot while at the wheel of his truck. Serafina loses the baby and her life is transformed. She becomes disoriented and on her daughter Rosa's high school graduation night two women maliciously tell her of her late husband's affair with Estelle Hohengarten. From that moment, she is demented, intent on protecting Rosa's 'innocence' in the presence of the young sailor who is courting her, and being far more assiduously courted *by* her. Caught between guarding Rosa's virginity and the need to reject what she has been told concerning Rosario, she beseeches the Virgin to 'give me a sign' that what she has been told about her husband is untrue.

Alvaro, also a banana truck driver, arrives. He reminds her in so many ways of the dead Rosario. He even has a rose tattoo, although it proves a contrivance, something he has had put on only that night. 'I wanted to be—close to you . . . to make you—happy', he insists when she discovers the falsity of his behaviour. She attempts to force him to take her to the Square Roof, where Rosario's supposed liaison with Estelle took place. He refuses, but has the fact confirmed on the telephone, following which Serafina shatters the urn containing her late husband's ashes.

Afer a series of contrivances involving Serafina, Rosa and Jack, her sailor, and Alvaro, who spends the night before being cast out, Serafina again feels the burning of the rose on her breast. 'I know what it means', she reflects. Alvaro is heard returning and she starts towards him.

The Rose Tattoo is, if anything, even more melodramatic than *Menagerie* and *Streetcar* and without the dimension of character and plot of either. Speaking of neighbouring housewives, Serafina declares its theme: 'Instead of the heart, they got the deep-freeze in the house.' Williams clearly believes in the heart.

In the pretentious *Camino Real*, the heart becomes an actual one, that of Kilroy, enlarged and defective. The artificiality and heavy-handedness extend even to the foreword of the published version: 'More than any other work that I have done, this play has seemed to me like the construction of another world, a separate existence . . . Its people are mostly archetypes of certain basic attitudes

and qualities with those mutations that would occur if
they had continued along the road to this hypothetical
terminal point in it.'

Camino Real, Williams' most obvious attempt at
expressionism, with its patsy who becomes a hero, may
rank as the most sentimental of his major plays. It certainly does not rank among the best of them.

It is, in fact, difficult to view *Camino Real* as other than
simply a bad play, a play that in all likelihood would have
found it very difficult to achieve production had its
author not previously twice received the New York
Drama Critics Circle Award.

In the prologue, Don Quixote de la Mancha, 'dressed
like an old "desert rat",' appears to announce, among
other things, one of Williams' recurrent themes: 'When
so many are lonely as seem to be lonely, it would be in-
excusably selfish to be lonely alone.'

But all, or virtually all, the major characters in the play
are lonely—and to a large extent 'lonely alone'
—whether they be identified as 'legendary' (Jacques
Casanova, Marguerite Gautier, Lord Byron and others)
or contemporary. Each is fleeing from himself, from the
past and from the present, and it does not require the ob-
viousness of Williams' labelling the plane many of them
are awaiting the Fugitivo to remind the audience that
they are yet another embodiment of his 'fugitive kind',
people prevented from escaping from the small port
town, people who are also at least a little afraid to escape.

Kilroy, the ex-Golden Gloves boxing champ, still with
his gloves, is another of Williams' poet figures. He is
bewildered by the behaviour of the others, from the hotel
proprietor to the all too obvious death-symbolizing
street cleaners, and is set up and set down, the victim.
Around him, the purple prose and the symbolism
abound: 'There is a time for departure even when there's
no certain place to go!' proclaims Byron. There is also
tenderness, 'the violets in the mountains . . . can break
the rocks if you believe in them and allow them to grow',
Jacques tells Marguerite. 'Time betrays us and we betray
each other', she responds. Williams even goes so far as to
have a gypsy tell Kilroy: 'We're all of us guinea pigs in the
laboratory of God. Humanity is just a work in progress.'

Not even Kilroy, the outsider, is permitted to escape
the verbal voluptuousness: 'I pity the world and I pity the
God who made it', he asserts toward the end. Perhaps the
worst of it comes as La Madrecita holds the body of

Kilroy, whom she has rescued from the lurking streetcleaners. Symbolism and allegory can become only so obvious before becoming ludicrous. 'This was thy son, America—and now mine. . . . Think of him, as he was before his luck failed him. Remember his time of greatness, when he was not faded, not frightened.' Kilroy, whose 'heart's solid gold', revives, snatching that heart back from the medical instructor; 'stewed, screwed and tattooed on the Camino Real', he is thinking of 'going *on* from—here!' One cannot help but wish he had thought of it considerably sooner.

Walter Kerr has written, in *How Not to Write a Play*, that in *Camino Real* Williams is 'analyzing his play at the same time as he is writing it, or, rather, he is giving us the analysis without ever having written the play'. Although Williams insists in an afterword to the play that he is not a 'thinking playwright', but is 'permitted only to feel', one of the major difficulties with the play is that it *is* primarily an intellectual exercise. With its 'legendary' figures, its obtrusive and overwritten symbols, its lack of viable flesh-and-blood characters, it never breaks through to a point where the audience ceases to play intellectual party games and begins to feel.

Any relatively brief critical survey of Williams' work inevitably must skim over certain plays that in another context would warrant fuller attention. *Summer and Smoke* (1948), *Orpheus Descending* (1957), *Suddenly Last Summer* (1958), *Period of Adjustment* (1960), even *Sweet Bird of Youth* (1959), are regrettably among them. *Cat on a Hot Tin Roof* (1955), which ranks among Williams' major works, obviously is not.

Williams is one of those playwrights who continues to rework his plays long after they have closed. Sometimes they benefit, sometimes they do not. With the 'new' *Cat*, produced in 1974, his decision clearly was a good one.

Cat is one of Williams' most highly theatrical plays. Its major characters have vitality and, with the exception of the underwritten Brick, the ex-football hero and sports commentator, latent homosexual and active alcoholic, possess sufficient interest to hold the attention throughout, despite the play's unnecessary repetitiousness.

Brick's wife, Maggie the Cat, has gone to great lengths to break up his relationship with his former team-mate Skipper; not to mention to bed with Skipper in order to demonstrate the latter's homosexual nature. Now, however, Skipper is dead and Brick, outwardly blaming Maggie, inwardly blames himself and takes to the bottle, each day waiting for the little 'click' that will grant him peace.

With Brick's father, Big Daddy, dying of cancer, however, complications impose themselves on his brooding, all-day courtship of oblivion. For who is to inherit those '28,000 acres of the richest land this side of the Valley Nile'? Neither Big Daddy nor Big Mama, who are unaware of the terminal nature of his illness—who, indeed, have been told he is suffering from nothing more serious than a spastic colon—feel much inclined toward their conscientious but otherwise unappealing elder son, Gooper, and his brood mare of a wife, Mae. But Brick *does* drink; he and Maggie have no children, a fact endlessly harped upon by Mae and her brood of 'no-necked monsters', as Maggie aptly describes them.

Williams attempts to keep too many balls in the air at one time for the play to be completely successful. On the one hand, there is Big Daddy, who tragically and too late has discovered that he has disliked his wife for years and now wants both a final fling, which he is destined not to have, and an heir from Brick. Then there is the guilt-ridden Brick, asserting the purity of his friendship with the dead Skipper, refusing to acknowledge it for what it was—for at least one of them—and because of that refusing also to go to bed with his wife. What of Maggie herself? Are her intensity and passion prompted more by a craving for wealth or a craving for Brick, even at the moment at the end of the play when she denies him his liquor, telling the hobbling, crutch-bound man she will return it only after he impregnates her, after which they'll 'get drunk together'?

Holding it all together should be two factors: the theme of 'mendacity', the curse that Brick tells his father is responsible for his alcoholism, and Brick himself. The mendacity theme emerges with considerably greater effect in the revised version, presumably thanks to restorations from the original text. It is seen to pervade virtually all the relationships, virtually all the major moments of confrontation, whether they have to do with Brick's relationship with Skipper, the impending death of Big Daddy or the vying for those 28,000 acres. For Brick has denied not only his guilt concerning Skipper, but Skipper himself; by doing so he has become an attractive nonentity, a fading shadow of the golden boy's promise (which, unfortunately, in itself is by now something of a cliché). Big Daddy must be kept from the truth—and not only out of kindness—save in an explosive confrontation with Brick.

Through it all the audience is asked to take on faith whatever it is that Maggie, Big Daddy and Big Mama find so attractive, so worthy of love, even of admiration, in Brick. The character is far too sketchily written for that. It is not sufficient to have Maggie remind that Brick is one of those 'weak, beautiful people who give up with such grace'—especially when the grace is not on view—and to witness instead only his ironically polite indifference. Brick is far too pivotal to everyone else's actions for that.

For the new version, Williams has dropped the Elia Kazan-inspired third act, leaving something both closer to his original and more ambiguous. He does, however, have Big Daddy return to tell his celebrated elephant story (deemed too ribald for the Broadway of 1955) and to indicate a more obvious complicity with Brick in Maggie's assertion of her fictitious pregnancy, her 'present' to the dying Big Daddy. In the revised text, Brick simply mutters 'Jesus!' when she tells of it, where on Broadway he had supported her. The play ends with the restoration of one of Williams' favourite lines (it occurs twice in the play), in response to Maggie's declaration of love: 'Wouldn't it be funny if that was true?'

Otherwise, the homosexual element and the language are more explicit and various lines have been clarified, updated or restored, almost always to positive effect. After two decades, and especially given what was a generally impressive 1974 production, the play holds up remarkably well.

The Night of the Iguana won the New York Drama Critics Circle Award in 1961, the last Williams play to do so. Set in a 'rather rustic and very Bohemian hotel' in Mexico, in 1940, it brings together yet another group of Williams' outcasts.

The Reverend Shannon is a defrocked Episcopal priest, now reduced to escorting tour groups for a third-rate travel agency. The current group of eleven is from a Baptist school in Texas and he has gone to bed with one of them, a seventeen-year-old vocal prodigy, to the distinct disapproval of her very 'butch' coach, who is determined to have Shannon fired.

Shannon is at the end of his rope, on the brink of one of his periodic breakdowns, two of which have occurred at this very hotel, as the recently widowed proprietress is at considerable pains to remind him, all the while attempting to get him in bed with her. As she notes: 'We've both reached a point where we've got to settle for something that works for us in our lives—even if it isn't on the highest kind of level.'

The next arrivals are Hannah Jelkes, who has been wandering the world with her ninety-seven-year-old grandfather, Nonno, 'the world's oldest living and practicing poet', and Nonno himself. They are penniless and Maxine insists they must leave in the morning. Hannah is the reverse of Maxine: virginal, withdrawn, 'artistic'. If anyone can help Shannon, it is probably she. Eager neither to possess him nor to destroy him, she knows that there can be 'broken gates between people so they can reach each other, even if it's just for one night only', in which there is 'a little understanding exchanged between them'.

Shannon and Hannah give verbal direction to the play's dominant symbol, the iguana who has been caught by the young Mexican houseboys and tied beneath the verandah to be fattened up for juicier eating and is trying desperately to scramble away. It is, Shannon says, 'trying to go on past the end of its goddam rope? Like *you*! Like *me*! Like Grampa with his last poem!' Hannah insists that he cut the iguana loose and he does, though he is at Maxine's mercy. 'I am at her disposal.' He does it 'because God won't do it'.

For Shannon and Hannah it has been a modern version of John of the Cross's dark night of the soul. For Nonno, the final night of all, for with his poem at last completed, he dies. Hannah is alone. Shannon will remain with Maxine to 'take care of the women' who accompany the men she can 'make the place attractive to'. He will not be 'happy', but neither, perhaps, will he be so haunted by his 'spook', by a God that failed.

The same overdrawn and over-emphasized symbols that mark virtually all Williams' plays appear again in *The Milk Train Doesn't Stop Here Anymore*, in which the poet Chris Flanders, who has earned the title 'Angel of Death', arrives at the villa of Mrs Goforth on Italy's *Divina Costiera* on the first of 'the two final days of Mrs Goforth's existence'. Like Chance Wayne in *Sweet Bird of Youth*, and others, he is one of Williams' attractive but aging young men, living off others, but also giving them a certain life.

As Chris appears, Mrs Goforth, who has spent the

summer working on her memoirs, has just been dictating recollections of her beloved Alex. And, as she tells her secretary, Blackie, 'I do need male company . . . that's what I need to be me, the old Sissy Goforth.' So Chris is settled in 'the little pink guest house', thence to take up his pre-ordained role. He reminds Blackie: 'I've had a good bit of experience with old dying ladies, scared to death of dying . . . and I've discovered it's possible to give them, at least to offer them, something closer to what they need than what they think they still want.' He gives her a mobile he has made and calls 'The Earth Is a Wheel in a Great Big Gambling Casino', presumably Williams' symbol for cosmic—God's—indifference to the fate of the individual. It is hardly the first time the playwright has given a character such sentiments. They receive their most obvious enunciation in Sebastian's idea of God in *Suddenly Last Summer*, in which he describes a beach 'all alive' with sea turtles engaged in a frantic dash toward the sea. But the birds sweep down on them, 'turning them over to expose their soft undersides, tearing the undersides open and rending and eating their flesh. Sebastian guessed that possibly only a hundredth of one percent of their number would escape to the sea'.

Chris is not really a negative force. Although he has a reputation for 'coming to call on a lady just a step or two ahead of the undertaker', he comes to bring them not merely to death but through it. With him on hand, they are permitted to die honestly. 'Death is one moment', he reflects, 'and life is so many of them.'

Mrs Goforth (whose name offers another of Williams' laboured symbols: 'It's my turn, now, to go forth') resists Chris until very near the end. But she *is* dying and she knows it, finally beseeching him: '*Don't leave me alone till*—', to which he responds, 'I never leave till the end.' He removes her rings and places them 'under her pillow like a Pharaoh's breakfast waiting for the Pharaoh to wake up hungry'. But Sissy Goforth has gone forth and now so can Christopher ('Christ-bearer'), 'Angel of Death'.

As the symbols have proliferated and become increasingly obvious, the attempts at the 'poetic' more laboured, the plays have deteriorated, providing a reminder that although Williams was originally hailed for exactly those qualities, it was his early characters —Amanda, Blanche, Maggie and others—who exercised the real appeal. This failing is particularly true of *Kingdom of Earth* (1968), *In the Bar of a Tokyo Hotel* (1969) and *Out Cry* (1973), somewhat less so of *Small Craft Warnings*, a 1972 revision of the earlier one-act *Confessional*.

There are some fine things in *Tokyo Hotel*, lines that recall the poignance and poetry of *Glass Menagerie*, moments that reveal Williams grappling with his intractable soul in the way the true artist on occasion must. There are also moments that suggest Williams' fear that the theatre of today is one far removed from the one that gave him his great triumphs, moments when he seems to reach for a style that is more 'with it', introducing, then just as quickly discarding, elements of studied, almost Pinteresque ambiguity, lines left dangling and unfinished and experimentation with spatial relationships—none of which have anything to do with what he has on occasion done so well.

The play is set in the Tokyo bar of the title and its plot is scant. Indeed, one of its most basic flaws is the fact that what occurs on stage is primarily a recounting of the crises, discoveries and frustrations that have occurred before the curtain rose. Mark, a wealthy and well-regarded painter, is already in the final stages of a spiritual and physical collapse. Pursuing experimental techniques which literally terrify him, he has arrived at an 'absolute oneness' in his work and self. His commitment and intensity are such that he has been almost consumed by them.

Williams has said that the play is 'about the usually early and peculiarly humiliating doom of the artist . . . and as death approaches, he hasn't the comfort of feeling any conviction that any of his work has had any essential value'. Nor has he any comfort from his wife of fourteen years. A typical Williams' 'heroine'—flamboyantly promiscuous, indifferent to her husband's needs, mocking, venomous—Miriam wants nothing more than to send him back to enter a sanitorium in the States, while she goes about her pleasures, among them the casual seduction of a reluctant young Japanese barman and a mysterious trip to Kyoto. Meanwhile, she refers to his paintings as 'circus-coloured mudpies'. By the time Mark's art dealer and friend flies in from New York at Miriam's request, it is already much too late for him either to be saved or to save himself. He collapses and dies in the bar-room, leaving Miriam momentarily 'released', but with a dawning recognition of the void that accompanies that release. She, too, seems fated to a role as one of Williams' lost souls.

In a sense the play is a sustained cry of agony, a testimony to Mark's assertion that, 'An artist has to lay his life on the line.' As such, it is almost inevitably without any normal ebb and flow of dramatic intensity, without sustained momentum. Occasionally, there are brief flashes of the poetry that once seemed to come so easily, but more often there is a shallow and pretentious profundity, an inability to communicate anything beyond the most superficial of insights. At times, it is almost embarrassing, as with 'The circle of light is the approving look of God . . . There's a limit to the circle of light. It's dangerous to step outside it'.

In general, *Small Craft Warnings* avoids that degree of excess. It is set in a beach-front bar on the Southern California coast, its denizens are the lonely and the losers, the drifters and the disheartened. They know each other; they spend all—and probably every—evening at Monk's Place, drinking their beer and their bourbon and their brandy, getting through life as best they can. It is simply a matter of survival.

Of them, only Leona, an itinerant beautician, possesses any vitality either as an individual or theatrically. As she rambles boozily on, on this the anniversary of the 'death-day' of her young brother, there is one thing she knows, one certainty she insists upon: 'Everyone needs! One beautiful thing! In the course of a lifetime! To save the heart from corruption! . . . Without one beautiful thing in the course of a lifetime, it's all a deathtime.'

There are few beautiful things in the lives of those at Monk's Place. One by one, in soliloquies lifted out of time, they tell their stories: the doctor who has been prevented from practising by his alcoholism and has turned abortionist; the forty-seven-year-old short-order cook; the homosexual script writer with his young blond pickup from Iowa; the sex-starved hooker, Violet; a male sex-object who has been sharing Leona's trailer; the bartender himself, living in fear of another heart attack, a final heart attack, in the night.

At its best, the play has considerable poignance and eloquence; at its worst it is banal, sentimental and tedious, attenuated to a point that tries the patience. It is a drama almost completely devoid of dramatic momentum, dominated by the literary self-indulgence of several

of the long monologues that are its reason for being.
Even that is not the real problem. The real problem is that
the characters themselves are more clichés than inherently interesting or believable. We have seen them in bar-
room plays almost without number—in *The Iceman
Cometh*, in Saroyan, in Charles Gordone's *No Place to Be
Somebody*—and in earlier Williams' works. *Small Craft
Warnings* adds almost nothing to our knowledge of them
as human beings, reveals no new dimensions. Quentin,
the older of the homosexuals, asks: 'What is the thing you
mustn't lose in this world before you're ready to leave it?'
then answers his own question: 'Surprise . . . the capacity
for being surprised.' There are no surprises in *Small Craft
Warnings*, only echoes from the past.

Out Cry would rank very high in any listing of Williams'
'worst' plays, it is static, dull almost to the point of
deadening.

Felice and Clare are brother and sister. As *Out Cry*
opens, they are on the stage of a deserted theatre. Or are
they? Is this the play within a play, the exercise in
Pirandello, the surface suggests? Are Felice and Clare
simply going to present the only play their present circumstances—they have been deserted by their company,
which considers them insane—will permit? A spiral
stairway leads to nowhere; a large, undefined black
sculpture stands upstage; there is a free-standing door, a
piano, odds and ends of furniture, a pile of cushions on
the floor.

'Clare, you are going to play Clare', Felice tells her.
And that is what she does. Throughout, *Out Cry* seems not
so much a play within a play as a reality that demands the
pretence of being a play. Felice and Clare *are* insane; they
think, or pretend to think, they are on a stage, are the
'deranged children of a false mystic' who has killed his
wife and himself.

Admittedly, this is pure supposition, for Williams
never makes it clear. Act 2 drags on from there, through
abortive attempts to break out of the room—the
prison—they are in, the too obviously symbolic blowing
of bubbles: 'Madness has a funny side to it, Clare. We
can't turn back to children before people.' But: 'The
worst thing that's transpired in our lives is being aware of
what's going on in our lives.'

Towards the end, it is suggested that the *Two Character
Play* that Felice and Clare ostensibly are performing is
'too personal, too special for audiences'. This seems to

me both true and something of a cop-out, a gesture of self-protection. *Out Cry* is intensely personal, perhaps the most personal play Williams has written, and there seems ample justification for considering Felice and Clare as two aspects, two parts, of Williams himself.

Those two parts finally come together. The play does not. It searches about, seeks a style, a mode of expression, but in the end is a victim of its own inertia.

In *Orpheus Descending*, Val Xavier, who functions as both Orpheus and Christ, another of Williams' symbolic, semi-mythical figures, observes: 'Nobody ever gets to know *no body*! We're all of us sentenced to solitary confinement inside our own skins, for life!' In *The Eccentricities of a Nightingale*, a revision of *Summer and Smoke*, Alma refers to 'my little company of the faded and frightened and difficult and odd and lonely'. Whether they be failed artists or poets, priapic young men or people of 'refinement' (Blanche, for instance), 'mad' (as most of Williams' heroines to some extent are) or mutilated, his characters are in some sense outsiders, struggling against a world that fails to recognize their vision or their 'talent'. They are attempting to escape from that very 'world of reality' from which, at fourteen, Williams wrote in the foreword to *Sweet Bird of Youth*, he was attempting to escape, although they seldom if ever fully succeed. They are offered not as victims of their private illusions, but victims of that world in which 'normality, triumphant, is nonetheless somehow damnable'. When Williams successfully presents their pain as people rather than as symbols, as he did in several of the early plays, he is a dramatist of poignance and power. When, however, he seeks to render it in non-realistic terms, in symbols that speak in capital letters, he at times becomes almost laughable, at others tedious. Regrettably, that has been all too often the case in more recent years.

3 Arthur Miller

Arthur Miller's reputation rests on far fewer plays than that of Tennessee Williams, who has averaged virtually a play a year since his first New York production. In fact, there is a temptation to say it rests on *one* play, *Death of a Salesman*, and that neither what went before its presentation on Broadway in 1949 nor what has been written since has approached its level. This is both true and to a large extent inevitable. *Salesman* has few challengers for the title of 'best' American play since World War II.

Miller's first professionally produced play, *The Man Who Had All the Luck* (1944), closed after four performances on Broadway. Earlier, he had written for the Federal Theatre Project and the CBS and NBC radio networks. It was, however, with *All My Sons* (1947), which ran for nearly a year and received the New York Drama Critics Circle Award as the best play of the season, that he first obtained substantial recognition.

All My Sons, like several other Miller plays, has been dubbed 'Ibsenesque'. With this play the label is particularly appropriate. Joe Keller is nearing sixty, a successful businessman, a good husband and father. He embodies the then current American myth. He has little education; he has worked hard; he prizes and takes pride in his family; his private morality is impeccable, his professional one somehow separate from it. 'I'm in business, a man is in business', he attempts to explain at one point. During World War II, in a moment of panic over what would happen to his business if he did not, Joe Keller gave the order to ship cracked cylinder heads to the air force, which resulted in twenty-one planes crashing in Australia. Rather than take the blame, he shifted it to his weak partner, who was jailed. Now, time has passed; although his friends and neighbours do not accept the idea that he is innocent, they respect the fact that he has been 'smart'.

Joe Keller's world begins to fall apart on the arrival of

his dead son's fiancée, Annie, the daughter of his imprisoned ex-partner, who believes her father to be guilty. Larry had been reported missing in a wartime plane crash three years before, but Joe and his wife, especially his wife, have kept alive the idea that he is not dead. Joe's remaining son, Chris, intends to marry Annie. When he reveals this to his father, he is told: 'You marry that girl and you're pronouncing him [Larry] dead.' But Chris is determined. He will leave town—and his father's business—if necessary in order to wed Annie. So, his father agrees to help him in terms of telling his mother.

Like most Miller plays, however, *All My Sons* is not simply domestic drama. He is concerned with the elements of the American myth that cause an otherwise decent man, 'with the imprint of the machine-shop worker and boss still upon him', a man of relatively limited ambitions, to act as Joe Keller did.

It all comes into focus when Annie's brother, George, arrives, just after a visit to his father. He is determined that Annie should not marry Chris, and considers Joe, not his own father, culpable in the shipping of the parts. Of course he is right, though it takes considerable contrivance on Miller's part to bring it all to a culmination. Chris, now convinced of his father's guilt, denounces him and leaves. Joe is abject. Nothing, he tells his wife, is bigger than the relationship between father and son. 'If there's something bigger than that I'll put a bullet in my head.'

Kate, however, will not accept any of it, though she in fact knows it is true. Most of all she will not accept that Larry is dead. Annie is forced to show her a letter she had received from him shortly before his plane crashed, in which the young pilot, having read in the press of the accusations against his father, all but stated that he would deliberately crash in his next mission. As he put it, 'They'll probably report me missing.' It remains only for Chris to return to tell them he is leaving for good. Confronted with this, finally realizing the *why* of Larry's death—'I think to him they were all my sons. And I guess they were'—he goes into the house and shoots himself.

Miller is not really unsympathetic to Joe Keller. He does, however, insist that there is a world beyond Joe's—his world with a 'forty-foot front, it ended at the building line'—a 'universe of people outside', as Chris tells his mother, 'and you're responsible to it'.

The message is unexceptionable, the method at this

remove far too predictable and clichéd, arising not out of character but principally through the contrivance of Larry's letter. Unlike most other Miller plays, *All My Sons* receives relatively few productions today (though there was a brief Off Broadway run in 1974, presumably in the wake of Watergate's revival of a consciousness of public ethics and morality). It would, largely because of the patness of its dramaturgy, seem a play whose time has passed, though the validity of its theme clearly has not.

Death of a Salesman, which won both the Drama Critics Circle Award and the Pulitzer Prize, is considerably richer in both theme and character, a play that employs expressionism as well as realism. As the years pass, it takes on dimension rather than diminishing.

It is now over twenty-five years since an actor playing Willy Loman, carrying two oversize sample cases, stepped on to a stage, crossed wearily to a doorway, passed through a kitchen, and deposited his burden in the living room. 'I'm tired to the death', he admitted. 'I couldn't make it. I just couldn't make it, Linda. I have such thoughts, I have such strange thoughts.'

At first glance, the disintegration of Willy Loman, the 'hard-working drummer who landed in the ash can like all the rest of them', seems curiously old-fashioned and trite. It deals not with cataclysms or cataclysmic issues, not even with abstract metaphysical questions in which each member of the audience may find something of the dilemma of his own existence. It is a play about a 'little boat looking for a big harbor', and few of us—at least in our own eyes—are 'little boats'. As past and present glide into each other, become at times almost interchangeable, Willy is recognizable as both victim and victimizer, a man who dreamed impossible dreams, passed them on to his two sons and, at sixty-three, is involved in a desperate struggle not to 'go out the way he came in . . . to add up to something'.

When *Salesman* opened, Harold Clurman called it 'a challenge to the American dream'. And perhaps that is what it was. Perhaps it still is. The friends and buyers who welcomed Willy Loman's visits, who could always somehow find an order for him, have died or retired. The salesman who once could make six or seven Boston calls in one day is now exhausted by one or two, and even those fail to provide him with sales. He can drive seven hundred miles and not make a cent. He talks to himself; he has fantasies. He has tried to commit suicide. The once premier road man of the company has been reduced to working on straight commission. Without a salary, he is forced to borrow fifty dollars a week from a man he scorns. Willy Loman, who placed so much store in being 'well liked', is lost in a generation of strangers, in a system alien to his previous years with the company.

'How long can that go on?' his wife Linda demands of his two sons, the one a self-deluding ladies' man, an about-to-make-it-big man who never will, the other a personable ex-football star, Willy's pride and the repository of his hopes, now in his thirties, a drifter destroyed by a moment when belief in his father's dreams of glory, the conviction that there but for the grace of God went God, fell victim to his inability to accept Willy's infidelity. 'I don't say he's a great man', Linda tells Biff. 'Willy Loman never made a lot of money. His name was never in the paper. He's not the finest character that ever lived. But he's a human being, and a terrible thing is happening to him. So attention must be paid. He's not to be allowed to fall into his grave like an old dog. Attention, attention must finally be paid to such a person.'

To some extent, Willy Loman's entire life has been a lie, a facade erected over long years in which he has accepted an illusion, more accurately, a delusion. In one sense, there is no Willy Loman. There is the smile, the handshake, the joke, the slap on the back. Willy believes his lie, believes it to the end. He cannot let himself do otherwise. If he does, his final sacrifice to it—the suicide that he tells himself will provide Biff with the insurance money to realize that impossible dream, that will free *him* from the danger of the mis-step that might reveal its error—will itself be meaningless. 'What are you building?' asks Willy's millionaire brother. 'Lay your hand on it. Where is it?'

In his introduction to the collected plays, Miller has written that Willy 'has broken a law without whose protection life is insupportable if not incomprehensible to him and to many others; it is the law which says that a failure in society and in business has no right to live'. Having broken that law, he pays the penalty. But if Willy's values have somewhere run amok, the play suggests, then those of the society that nurtured them have done no less. It is a society that has given up substance for surface, one that hardly knows what substance is. Man is only as real as his realities, but, if he indeed is the stuff that dreams are made of, they, no less, are what he is made of. In the conflict between those realities and those dreams, Willy Loman finds his existence—and his reason to die.

In one form or another, *Death of a Salesman* encompasses nearly everything that Miller did before, nearly everything he has done since. It revolves around what has been one of his continuing themes—in *The Man Who Had All the Luck*, in *All My Sons*, in *The Price*—the relationship between fathers and sons, the relationship between brothers. (When *The Price* was produced in 1968, he described it as, 'in terms of theme, an outgrowth of *Salesman*'.) It contains, too, his obsession with man's obligation to assume responsibility. (There is a sense in which Miller's entire dramatic output might be summarized under the heading 'No Man Is an Island'.) In *All My Sons*, Chris tells his father 'You have a talent for ignoring things'. In *After the Fall*, Quentin is obsessed with his responsibility in Maggie's suicide; the Austrian prince in *Incident at Vichy* with his culpability in the Nazi atrocities against the Jews. 'It is necessary', Miller has written, 'if one is to reflect reality, not only to depict why a man does what he does, or why he nearly didn't do it, but why he cannot simply walk away and say to hell with it.' All this, in embryo at least, exists in *Salesman*.

For a moment, however, one should perhaps step aside and look at Arthur Miller in the context of his times, in relation to the social, cultural and political forces that have shaped his outlook. Born in Manhattan, on 17 October, 1915, of a family his friend and colleague Harold Clurman has described as 'unequivocally middle-class and Jewish', he attended elementary school in Harlem and high school in Brooklyn. Though he was not a devout practising Jew, he acknowledges that he did absorb 'a certain viewpoint—a commitment to the continuity of life and the need to go on even though there is tragedy in the world'. This feeling was to find its echo in such plays as *Incident at Vichy* (1964), which deals with what Miller calls a 'literal situation as well as the moral and ethical situations [in which a group of people] are faced with the need to respond to total destruction'.

In the first volume of *Theatre*, the abortive annual of the Repertory Theatre of Lincoln Center (which produced *After the Fall* and *Incident at Vichy*), Clurman wrote that 'Miller is a moralist. A moralist is a man who believes he possesses the truth and aims to convince others of it. In Miller this moralistic trait stems from a strong family feeling. In this context, the father as prime authority and guide is central . . . to his sons he is the personification of Right and Truth. . . . The shock which shatters Miller's dramatic cosmos always begins with the father's inability to enact the role of moral authority the son assigns to him and which the father willy-nilly assumes. . . . Both may be innocent, but both suffer guilt.'

This is no less true in *The Price* than in *Salesman* and in other of the early works. Apart from *Incident at Vichy*, the one major play in which it does not appear in some guise or some degree is *The Crucible* (1953), which in its way is quite the most remarkable and interesting of Miller's works, though not his 'best play'. It is remarkable not merely because it is his lone historical drama, but because it is the one that, despite its seventeenth-century trappings, probably was the precursor of his considerably more recent personal (as opposed to theatrical) political activism.

The Crucible is, in a sense, Miller's most 'committed' play. Its flaws are largely the product of that very commitment. Nominally, it deals with the hysteria, self-serving accusations and hypocrisy of the Salem witch trials of 1692, in fact with a situation, a state of mind, that has recurred throughout history. At the time it was produced on Broadway in January, 1953, McCarthyism was a blot on the American conscience. (It is worth noting, however, that it was not until 1956 that Miller himself was found guilty of contempt of Congress for his refusal to answer questions of the, now defunct, House Un-American Activities Committee, a charge of which he was later cleared.)

Miller has said that it was not only McCarthyism that moved him to write the play, but 'the fact that a political, objective, knowledgeable campaign from the far Right was capable of creating not only a terror, but a new subjective reality, a veritable mystique which was gradually assuming even a holy resonance. [The terror people experienced] was being knowingly planned and consciously engineered, and yet all they knew was terror. That so interior and subjective an emotion could have been so manifestly created from without was a marvel to me. It underlies every word in *The Crucible*'. The play's theme, he concludes, 'was the handing over of conscience to another . . . and the realization that with conscience goes the person'.

Reaction to the Broadway production was mixed. A subsequent Off Broadway version was received more enthusiastically, quite possibly because the national climate had considerably altered. Not altogether surprisingly, Miller himself feels that a non-American production—at the British National Theatre in January, 1965—has most completely realized what he was attempting. 'Olivier's production is the best I've seen', he said in an interview. 'Mainly because the characters are approached as human beings, and the life of the town as a strong force rather than some generalized movement. The people behave as though they worked on farms—the acting is beautiful.'

It was not really a question of acting, at least not in essence. It was a question of context, of twelve years in time and of an ocean in geography. Although the National Theatre's programme alluded to the McCarthy era (and contained a brief excerpt from a 1950 McCarthy speech), the play was permitted to stand on its own, a commentary on the times no doubt, but not a prisoner of them. Miller's recurrent plea, here seen in the person of John Proctor in struggle with himself and the system that is trying to bring him down in the witchcraft proceedings, the plea that man is responsible for his actions and can neither abdicate that responsibility nor disown the consequences, surfaced as *The Crucible* became a drama that was narrowly political only in analogy. We all have witch-hunts. Miller became what he always has been, a playwright 'constantly awed by what an individual is . . . by the possibilities he has for any betrayal, any cruelty, as well as any altruism, any sacrifice'.

In *A View from the Bridge* (1956), Miller explores those 'possibilities for any betrayal'. John Proctor, the hero of *The Crucible*, in the last act asks: 'How may I live without my name?' Eddie Carbone, the longshoreman whose apartment in the Red Hook section of Brooklyn provides the scene for most of the play's action, dies begging one of the men he has betrayed to 'gimme my name'. Before that, he has gone through a long series of anxious and agonizing moments.

Eddie and his wife, Beatrice, have for years brought up Catherine, the daughter of Beatrice's deceased sister. She has been virtually their daughter. Now, suddenly, she is a young woman, about to take a secretarial job. It is, of course, to mark a distinct change in Eddie's and Catherine's relationship and he does not welcome it. But, that very night, two 'submarines', illegal immigrants from Italy, Beatrice's cousins, are to arrive and all else must take second place to ensuring their safety. Eddie is at pains to warn Catherine of the necessity for secrecy, to remind her of the punishment meted out—and due—to an informer. 'Just remember, kid, you can quicker get back a million dollars that was stole than a word you gave away.'

But Catherine falls in love with one of the 'submarines', the young, blond Rodolpho, and Eddie is enraged. Rodolpho sings, he can design dresses, do other things that Eddie insists 'ain't right' in a man. He contends that the young man is homosexual, though he can come no closer than 'ain't right' to the word, and that Rodolpho is simply after the opportunity for citizenship that marriage to Catherine will afford. Then, one night, he returns home drunk and finds them together. Insisting that Rodolpho leave, he kisses each of them on the mouth in a clumsy, but demeaning attempt to show the young man's homosexuality. A few days later he calls the Immigration Bureau to report anonymously the presence of Marco and Rodolpho. When the officers arrive, Marco, who is thirty-two and in the States only to make sufficient money to support his impoverished family, *knows*. He publicly accuses Eddie, renders him pariah in a neighbourhood in which the code, the rules and prejudices of an older society remain. Eddie has violated them and Eddie will die in a struggle with the soon-to-be-deported Marco (though through his own knife).

Before that, however, Beatrice has confronted Eddie with the truth of his treachery, the fact that he has wanted something he could not have: Catherine, and that it is that that has lead him to his violation of the Calabrian code he himself fully believes in. Alfieri, a lawyer who acts as something of a Greek chorus, would seem to embody Miller's own view in his remarks on 'the awesomeness of a passion which . . . despite even its destruction of the moral beliefs of the individual, proceeds to magnify its power over him until it destroys him'.

Eddie himself has not really known his motivation. He has at all times been able to convince himself that he was acting in Catherine's best interests, not out of what is in effect an incestuous desire for her, their relationship having for practical purposes been that of father and daughter. What Miller says of Eddie, though its validity is at first glance questionable, is to some extent true of virtually all his early heroes. 'He possesses or exemplifies the wondrous and humane fact that he too can be driven to what in the last analysis is a sacrifice of himself for his conception, however misguided, of right, dignity and justice.'

That is certainly true of Von Berg, the Austrian nobleman in *Incident at Vichy*, a play that in virtually every other way falls outside the Miller *oeuvre*.

The scene is 'a place of detention' in occupied Vichy, France, in 1942. Several men have been picked up and brought in, reason unknown—but sensed. All, some more obviously than others, are Jews, the subject of the Nazis' Final Solution. All, that is, but Von Berg. The fact that he is there—and obviously not a Jew—when combined with the release of a businessman, gives them a false hope, or at least the pretence of one.

One by one, they are called into the office and disappear. The German Major who is nominally in charge is clearly disturbed. A line officer who has been wounded and sent to Vichy while he recuperates, he says to one of the captives, 'This is as inconceivable to me as it is to you.' But, in the end, he *will* do his 'duty', will turn aside one of the men's appeals to his better nature, his humanity.

There is a pretentiousness, a heavy-handedness, to *Incident at Vichy* that seriously weakens it. Leduc, a psychiatrist, observes to Von Berg: 'Each man has his Jew; it is the other' and at another point insists: 'It's your guilt I want, it's your responsibility.'

Von Berg will of course ultimately go free. He is there by virtue of a mistake (and another Miller contrivance). He has his interview, is given his white pass, which he gives to Leduc, who escapes. The final image is that of the German Major and Von Berg as they stand, 'forever incomprehensible to one another, looking into each other's eyes'. Had Miller been able to suggest more of that incomprehension, he would have written more of a play and less of a tract. It is not always enough to be on the side of the angels.

If *Incident at Vichy* is largely a tract, *After the Fall* (also 1964) is an exorcism, a confessional. Its action 'takes place in the mind, thought, and memory of Quentin', a lawyer in his forties, and it involves his wives and parents and friends who have been subpoenaed by the House Un-American Activities Committee. Principally, however, it involves Maggie, an intially dumb, childlike, switchboard operator who, mainly thanks to Quentin, becomes a highly successful singer. When he marries her,

his career becomes a victim. She absorbs all his attention—as Marilyn Monroe, whom Miller married in 1956
and divorced in 1961, apparently absorbed his. (He
wrote no plays during that period, only the script for the
film *The Misfits*, which starred Ms Monroe.) Their life
together is tumultuous, marked by her drinking and
suicide attempts and his attempts to reclaim her.

Miller, however, is trying to make a case for Miller (for
Quentin, one should say), trying to exonerate him of any
culpability in the consequences of his earlier political
associations and the suicide of Maggie, who idolized him.
He sees himself as wronged, will not acknowledge that he
may have been wronging. 'Is the knowing all?' he asks.
'To know, and even happily, that we meet unblessed; not
in some garden of wax fruit and painted trees, that lie of
Eden, but after, after the Fall, after many, many deaths.'
About all one can say of *After the Fall* is that it is a play any
playwright should be glad to have got out of his system.
Imposing it on an unsuspecting public is another matter.

With *The Price* (1968), Miller returned to safer, if more
clichéd, ground. In it, he probes to find the reality behind
the obsessions, lies and psychological necessities that
have kept two brothers apart for sixteen years and,
brought to flash-point, threaten one man's marriage and
the other's sanity. The critic for *Life* magazine went so far
as to call it a 'retrogressive play, half Ibsen, half Yiddish
theatre'. He was not far from right.

Miller himself contends that *The Price* is 'right down the
middle of our times', that in dealing with two brothers
who are attempting to 'make some sense of their lives' it
shows that 'certain things cannot be justified' on a quid
pro quo basis but must be the consequence of an act—or
the rejection of an act—of love.

The Manhattan brownstone that Police Sergeant Victor Franz once shared with his family is about to be torn
down. He returns in order to dispose of furniture and
other belongings that have been stored there over the
years. He is nearing fifty and about to retire from the
police force. As he awaits the appraiser, he reminisces
with his wife about the past and worries over the future.

The 1929 stock market crash had deprived his
previously well-to-do father of not merely his money but
of his self-confidence. While his brother, Walter, by now
a highly successful surgeon, continued his medical
studies and career (sending five dollars per month as his
contribution to his father's upkeep), Victor laid aside his

college career to minister to the old man's needs. Now, after nearly three decades of resentment and self-pity, his imminent retirement confronts him with what seems a partially wasted promise and a future of mounting uncertainty.

On the face of it, the story seems clear: the self-sacrificing brother and the self-serving one. Asked by the appraiser what he has against money, Victor reflects: 'Nothing, I just didn't want to lay down my life for it. But I think I laid it down another way, and I'm not even sure anymore what I was trying to accomplish.'

Walter has been asked to come to the apartment to join in disposing of the furniture. When he unexpectedly appears, the two men begin to thrash out their sixteen years of rancour, guilt and unspoken knowledge. Why had Walter neglected his seemingly needy father? Why had he then declined to give Victor the money necessary to complete his education?

Slowly the pattern of both their lives emerges. For Victor it has been a life in which he saw himself as Job, thereby excused from even those strides he might have taken. For Walter the early success has been shadowed by a failure in marriage and a three-year-long nervous breakdown.

As the conflict unfolds, it becomes clear that the question is not nearly so clear-cut as it at first appeared. For the father, in his fear, had been unwilling to spend several thousand dollars he indeed did have—a fact even then known to Walter. Thus, he had been able to keep Victor chained to him and had aborted his scientific career. Victor, in a sense, had been used as a shield against a world the older man could not face. Confronted with the fact—one he at least subconsciously has been partly aware of—Victor demands: 'What's the difference what you know? Do *you* do everything you know? . . . I thought if I stuck with him, if he could see that somebody was still . . . I can't explain it; I wanted to . . . stop it from falling apart.'

They continue to lacerate each other; Walter with 'realism' and a certain kind of reality. He tells Victor, 'We invent ourselves, Vic, to wipe out what we know. You invent a life of self-sacrifice, a life of duty; but what never existed cannot be upheld. . . . There was nothing here to betray. I am not your enemy.'

Thus it ends, with neither the victor, but both having paid the price of their decisions. In the published version of the play, Miller comments: 'As the world now operates, the qualities of both brothers are necessary to it; surely their respective psychologies and moral values conflict at the heart of the social dilemma.' Doubtless it is true, but Miller has not made a very persuasive case for it.

Nor has he made a particularly persuasive case for either God *or* Lucifer in *The Creation of the World and Other Business* (1972), his first attempt at a comedy, which ran on Broadway for only twenty performances.

Using the Book of Genesis as his background material, Miller was concerned with what the programme called 'three questions on the human dilemma': why, if God made everything and God is good, he made Lucifer; whether there is something in the way we are born that makes us want the world to be good and, most important to the Miller canon and the play: 'When every man wants justice, why does he go on creating injustice?'

To explore them, he takes Adam—a 'schmuck', as God calls him—from the creation of Eve through their discovery of sex, the eating of the apple, getting tossed out of Paradise and Cain's slaying of Abel. It is all very portentous, though there are occasional good comic moments, and the dialogue runs the gamut from the pseudo-poetic to Yiddish anachronisms. At times, there is a certain whimsical charm, but Miller's insights are anything but profound and his comedy insufficiently funny, with the result that it is more interesting in its aspirations than it is successful in their realization.

That is true of most Miller plays and it is difficult to avoid the conclusion that *Death of a Salesman* and perhaps *The Crucible* aside, his standing as one of the leading American playwrights since World War II is more the result of lack than of performance.

4 William Inge

It once was an almost automatic grouping. For the writer on the American theatre, 'serious' theatre, William Inge seemed to rank right up there with his two postwar contemporaries, Williams and Miller. The equation was a mistake, but an understandable one, in those brief, heady days when the American theatre seemed on the brink of an era of enormous creativity.

William Inge's tragedy—and doubtless a major contribution to his 1973 suicide—was that of a small talent hailed out of proportion, and even that on the wane within less than a decade. *Come Back, Little Sheba*, a huge success, was first produced in 1950; *A Loss of Roses*, his last work of any consequence (though it was a complete failure on Broadway), in 1959. After it came *Natural Affection* (1963) and *Where's Daddy?* (1966), but by then the American theatre had passed Inge by. His was not an uncommon experience and it may say more about the dearth of 'serious' American plays and playwrights than it is comfortable to acknowledge.

It may even say more about America, for Inge's early work, in particular, was that of the quintessential Midwesterner. Born in Kansas in 1913, he wrote of less complicated Americans in a less complicated time, people who lived by, and sometimes violated, values and ideals once commonly held. In other words, he reflected the values and ideals of his audience. Writing of what he calls 'the new Pineros', the American critic Gerald Weales says: 'Inevitably, in their attempts to get serious, they get sidetracked into sentiment, romance, theatrical and ideational cliché, but for a time at least, their new dressing of old bromides wins them commercial and critical success.'

Inge's first success came with the Broadway production of *Come Back, Little Sheba* (1950), and it is curious to note that here, as with Williams, Miller and Albee, the playwright's first major play is arguably his best play.

The Sheba of the title is a dog and, like youth and happiness, dreams dreamed and unredeemed, Sheba has 'just vanished—vanished into thin air'. Sheba is gone and the youth and high hopes of Lola and Doc, her attempting-to-recover alcoholic husband, are on the point of going over the brink if they are not already over it. Doc tells Lola that 'what's in the past can't be helped', that one has to live for the present. He might have been 'a big M.D.' today, instead of a chiropractor; they might have had a family, money, a nice house, had he not taken to 'gettin' drunk every night'. But he did, and now they have to 'keep on living . . . gotta keep goin' . . . somehow'.

Unfortunately, Marie, the young girl who is rooming with them, is being courted by The Athletic Turk and it arouses Doc's jealousy, causes him to go off the wagon on a multi-day drunk. On the night before it begins, aware of what is going on between the two young people, Lola can only call out, plaintively, lost in the dark that can come even before the top of the stairs: 'Come back, Little Sheba. Come back.'

In a foreword to one of the collections in which *Sheba* appears, Brooks Atkinson suggest that Lola and Doc 'survive a shattering crisis that will presumably stabilize their future', that each of them has learned something fundamental about the other. This seems dubious. Lola is a pathetic figure, lost and lonely, trying to ward off the inevitable; even so, she is a palpably believable one. Doc is not, and the marginal characters remain entirely that, marginal. In consequence, and despite the play's generally 'well-made' construction, it is a peculiarly period piece, and, if a period has passed, the play it leaves behind must offer more than the amateur Freudianism of *Sheba*. Intentions will seldom replace insights.

Picnic (1953) received both the Pulitzer Prize and the New York Drama Critics Circle Award. It is difficult to see why, save for the paucity of competition and the often quixotic behaviour of the judges.

In his foreword to *Four Plays*, Inge wrote: 'I deal with surfaces in my plays, and let whatever depths there are in my material emerge unexpectedly so that they bring something of the suddenness and shock which accompany the discovery of truths in actuality.' And surfaces, surfaces alone, are precisely what he deals with in *Picnic*.

Picnic is set in a Kansas town in the yard shared by Flo Owens and Helen Potts. Mrs Owens is a widow of about forty, with two daughters, artistic-tomboyish Millie, who is sixteen, and the beautiful Madge, eighteen. Helen Potts is a somewhat older woman, also a widow, who lives with, or is lived upon, by her invalid mother. Into their lives comes Hal, seemingly a vagabond, but in reality an ex-football star and fraternity brother of Madge's intended (by her mother) husband, the very wealthy Alan Seymour.

Events follow a relatively predictable course. The eager mother insists to her daughter that she be more avid in her attentions towards Alan: 'A pretty girl doesn't have long—just a few years in which she's the equal of kings and can walk out of a shanty like this and live in a palace with a doting husband who'll spend his life making her happy.'

But it is not to be. Millie becomes enchanted with the virile Hal; Hal and Madge fall in love. As the play ends, Madge is about to follow him to Tulsa. 'I guess you don't love someone because he's perfect', she tells her mother.

Nor do you necessarily love a play because its heart is in the right place, that of True Love. Some of *Picnic*'s dialogue is straight out of the afternoon soap operas and the worst of the women's magazines:

> FLO (*sinking down on her knees*): Darling, even if you do love him, try to forget it! Try!
> MADGE (*pulls away*): It's no use, Mom.
> FLO: Oh, God! Oh, God! . . . Helen! Helen! could I stop her?
> MRS POTTS: Could anyone have stopped you, Flo?

Although it may seem unfair to quote such a concluding scene out of context, this is the level of all too much of Inge's writing, though seldom—at least in the early quartet of successful plays—more obvious and recurrent than it is in the shallow and sentimental *Picnic*.

Bus Stop (1955), also set in a small Kansas town, is in some ways markedly better. At the very least, its characters, although remaining essentially clichés, possess more diversity and individuality.

A bus has been forced to stop for the night in Grace's restaurant. Outside, a blizzard is raging and the phone lines are down. Inside, it is dingy, with several small tables and a counter. Elma, the waitress, is a teenager, still in high school. Grace is, as Inge puts it, 'a more seasoned character in her thirties or early forties'.

Into their lives come a diverse sextet: Will Masters, the conscientious local sheriff; Cherie, a small-time *chanteuse* (or so she wants to be regarded); Bo Decker, the virginal—despite his boasting—young cowboy who wants to take her back to his ranch; Virgil Blessing, his guitar-playing buddy; Carl, the bus driver, who will share a bed with Grace; and Dr Gerald Lyman, an alcoholic former college professor who can spout Shakespeare at the drop of a hat and who utterly fascinates the young waitress.

By the time the bus is ready to leave the next morning, a number of things have happened in terms of their realizations and self-realizations. Bo and Cherie *will* go off to that ranch together, despite all the antagonisms they have experienced. Dr Lyman *won't* be joined by Elma in the city for a concert. He knows what he is, though she may not: 'My dear girl, I have disapproved of my entire life.' Grace and Carl *will* get together on his bus's next trip.

It isn't that *Bus Stop,* which Inge himself considered a comedy, is in any sense dreadful. It is good enough of its kind; its kind, however, is not good enough to last beyond its moment in time, and that time was a short one. It has been succeeded by other, doubtless equally unenduring, clichés and romanticisms. For that, as Congreve once reflected, is the way of the world. At least it is the way of the theatre.

The Dark at the Top of the Stairs (1957) was Inge's last success, either critical or commercial, and, if one can mourn the 'tragedy' of a skyrocketing career so brief as to be almost a firecracker, one can also see the reasons for the decline in this lavishly overpraised play.

In his introduction to *The Dark at the Top of the Stairs,* Tennessee Williams suggested that those who entered the theatre for the play 'enter to take comfortable seats by the fireside without anxiety, for there is no air of recent or incipent disorder on the premises'. He went on to describe Inge's talent as one 'for offering, first, the genial surface of common American life, and then not ripping but quietly dropping the veil that keeps you from seeing yourself as you are. Somehow he does it in such a way that you are not offended or startled by it. It's just what you are, and why should you be ashamed of it?'

This, however, is exactly what Inge does *not* do in *Dark*; at least in the latter part. Williams is most certainly correct in asserting that the audience will be 'comfortable'.

It is the 1920s, in a small town close to Oklahoma City. A flight of stairs leads off from the Floods' living room. At the top of those stairs is the dark hallway that gives the play its title. Inge's stage directions read: 'We are conscious of this area throughout the play, as though it holds some possible threat to the characters.'

Rubin Flood is a travelling salesman and times aren't good. As the play opens, he is about to set off on yet another selling trip—and having yet another row with his justifiably suspicious wife Cora. They have two children, the sixteen-year-old Reenie and ten-year-old Sonny. Sonny has been smothered with mother-love, is an object of scorn, a 'sissy', to his contemporaries. Indeed, about all he seems to have is his collection of movie star pictures and his talent at elocution. He tells his mother why *he* is afraid of the dark at the top of the stairs: 'Cause . . . you can't see what's in front of you. And it might be something awful.' That describes the underlying emotion not merely of most of the characters in *Dark*, but of many of the characters in virtually all of Inge's plays.

Reenie is shy and being pushed by her mother, who, unknown to Rubin, has bought her a fancy new dress to wear to a big birthday dance at the country club. When he inadvertently discovers it, it sets off yet another in their seemingly endless round of arguments and, this time, it is initially suggested, perhaps the final parting.

The real core of *Dark*, however, is the evolving relationship between Reenie, who begins to emerge from her shyness when she meets her blind-date, Sammy Goldenbaum, and Sammy and Sonny, who have an instant rapport. Sammy is a Jew, and terribly conscious of it. The son of a minor motion picture actress, he has been shunted off to good schools and, currently, to a military academy. Intelligent, considerate, well-mannered, likeable, he provides the play's sole drama. For, on the night of the dance, after being insulted about his Jewishness by the hostess, the tortured Sammy commits suicide. Because she didn't want him to consider her a 'wallflower', Reenie had introduced Sammy to the girl the party was being held for, telling him there was someone *she* had to talk to. Then she ran off to hide. It was at that point that the other girl's mother told Sammy she 'wasn't giving this party for Jews, and she didn't intend for her daughter to dance with a Jew, and besides, Jews weren't allowed in the country club anyway'. Sammy went looking for Reenie, but she was nowhere to be found.

It was not sufficient reason to commit suicide, of

course, but Sammy did. In the 'old blabbermouth', Cora comments, he probably heard what seemed to him 'the voice of the world'. And Reenie, by her absence, failed him, albeit unwittingly, when 'one or two words might have saved him'.

There is more to *Dark* than this, of course: the anguished confession of Cora's visiting sister Lottie that, contrary to Cora's opinion, her marriage has not been a happy one, that she was frigid: 'I never did enjoy it the way some women ... say they do', which led to the emasculation of her husband; the return of Rubin and the Floods' reconciliation. With that, the children, who have formerly battled tooth and nail, go off to the movies—together—and Cora climbs the stairs to join Rubin, who waits to take her to bed. Apart from Sammy, apparently everyone will live happily ever after, for such is the sentimental world of William Inge.

In an interview, Inge acknowledged, 'I guess I was the little boy. However, it was not an autobiographical play, but I did kind of base a piece of fiction around the members of my family. But they are only very vague resemblances to my family.' That, perhaps, is one of the difficulties: they are also only 'resemblances' to people. They analyse themselves and each other, but fail to display in their actions more than the most superficial manifestations of what lies at their core. It is far easier to talk about what one is or isn't than to reveal it dramatically through clashes or meshing of personalities, confrontations with situations. It is no accident that the decisive moments of *Dark*—the suicide and Rubin's decision to return home—take place offstage. As the curtain descends, Reenie has recognized her selfishness, Sonny has been informed he is now too old to share his mother's bed and Rubin and Cora are going back to sharing theirs. As a Freudian casebook it just might do; as a play of any enduring interest it will not.

After the string of successes that began with *Sheba* in 1950, Inge came upon far harder times, beginning with his last work of real interest, *A Loss of Roses*, in 1959.

'The production of *A Loss of Roses* was a complete failure', he wrote in his introduction to the published version. 'And yet, I have never gone into production with a play in which I had such complete confidence. Perhaps I was too confident of the play, for I could never really believe that it would not succeed until the last few days of our out-of-town engagement, when suddenly I realized that the play I had thought I had written was not happening on the stage. By that time, it was too late to make all the changes that would have been necessary. I tried to prevent its coming into New York but this would have brought me a greater personal financial loss than I could have handled. I have never felt so trapped. Finally, there was nothing to do but let the show come in, knowing that it would meet with failure, knowing that it could have been successful.'

I have quoted from Inge's introduction at length primarily because he seems to have been right. As published, if not as produced, *Roses*, the 'complete failure', verbose though it is, is every bit as good as some of the earlier 'successes'. If that is a relative distinction, it nonetheless possesses some significance in view of the entirely downhill path Inge's career was to follow from that time forward. Walter Kerr has written that its failure stemmed 'not from any momentary fatigue on the playwright's part but from a growing tendency in the conventional theatre . . . for the dramatist to work in an ever narrower range, and with an ever softer and more indulgent touch'.

Inge was not really working within any narrower range than he had been in *Sheba*, *Picnic*, *Bus Stop* and *The Dark at the Top of the Stairs*. The distortions that may have occurred in production aside, *Roses* is a completely typical Inge play.

There is seemingly an Oedipal relationship between Helen and her son Kenny. At least he cannot break away. Although he has been offered a much better job out of town, he has elected to remain as an attendant in a local filling station. Yet, he cries out, 'Quit bossing me all the time'. But, a moment later, when she has drawn back from his embrace: 'What's wrong with showing a little affection?' To which she responds: 'Maybe I'm *afraid* of needing you.'

Matters become appreciably more complicated with the arrival of Lila, an actress, friend and former semi-servant, who almost immediately becomes a substitute mother and object of his sexual desires for Kenny. He does, however, briefly rebel, insisting, 'I'm sick of women tending me and looking after me . . . I'm gettin' out.'

He doesn't, of course. Instead, he remains to 'take care of' Lila. On the morning after their liaison, however, he is having second thoughts about marrying her: 'Like, you may have been right in the first place, when you were telling me yesterday that things wouldn't work out for us. . . . I do like you an awful lot. It's just that, I realize now it wouldn't be right for us to be married.'

With that, Lila makes an ineffectual suicide attempt. Kenny admits he has done everything to spite his mother, acknowledging his jealousy ('Dad was the only man in this family you ever loved. Oh sure, *he* was the hero of this family. Not me'). To which Helen gives the answer that is presumably intended as the heart of Inge's play: 'I've loved you as much as I dared, son. . . . If I'd loved you any more, I'd have destroyed you.'

That admitted, Kenny decides to leave for a job in Wichita and Lila departs with her actor friend Ricky for a distinctly disreputable, though lucrative, career in the big city. She has lost the roses, the innocence, she recalls from her first day of school. She had given them to a teacher and she wanted them back, but that teacher shook her finger and said, 'when I gave away lovely presents, I couldn't expect to get them back. . . . There's still so many things I want back.'

There is, however, no genuine depth to *Roses*, any more than there is to most of Inge's previous plays. Instead, there is a typical Freudian situation, almost a casebook example, that one is asked to accept as 'real life'. Real life seldom, as we have more recently come to realize, appears as a casebook of the old sort. Even when it does, it exists on far more levels than in *Roses*. It's hardly a revelation for a character to admit she is 'emotionally immature'.

I have, I am aware, been far harder on Inge than on some of the other playwrights discussed in this book. He was, after all, an honest, hard-working craftsman. Although he was to write other plays after *Roses*, he never really recovered from that play's failure, which was not entirely his fault. The Broadway production problems aside, time had passed him by, the theatre had gone on to other things. Though he was to attempt to come closer to those things in his subsequent work, he could not make the adjustment, for his was a talent that, dealing 'with surfaces', in the end was unable to move beyond them. Knowing what we do today, it is far easier to speculate on *why* than it was at the time.

5 Edward Albee

Almost from the moment of his first New York production, *The Zoo Story* (1960), Edward Albee has been regarded as the most 'promising' American playwright since the Williams–Miller generation. With *Who's Afraid of Virginia Woolf?* (1962), the hopes and hosannas increased. Since, there has been mainly disappointment, a series of plays that fell short of effectiveness interspersed with adaptations of other writers' works. Was Albee, then, yet another flash-in-the-pan, a one-play playwright destined to the same fate as Inge, Anderson and all too many others? It would be easy to concur. Yet Albee (born in 1928) is still in his forties. His two most recent plays, *All Over* (1971) and *Seascape* (1975), while not successful on the level of *Virginia Woolf*, are among his most ambitious.

The Zoo Story takes place in Central Park. It is summer; it is the present and Peter is smoking a pipe, peacefully reading a book, when he is approached by Jerry. He is exactly what he appears to be: a young publishing executive (salary $18 000); one wife, two daughters, two cats, two parakeets and an apartment in Manhattan's East Seventies. He has, in short, all the prerequisites for a character in the Sloan Wilson grey-flannel-suit novels of the period.

Albee sets his theme early: Jerry tells Peter, 'I don't talk to many people—except to say like: give me a beer, or where's the john, or what time does the feature go on . . . You know—things like that. . . . But every once in a while I like to talk to somebody, really talk.'

Who does *talk* to many people? Peter is bewildered by the seeming lack of communication; yet communication, for him, exists only in the realm of the inconsequential. Repeated attempts by Jerry leave him only indifferent, visibly resentful that his afternoon's relaxation has been interrupted by this somewhat unkempt young man. He is unwilling to become involved on any level save the most superficial. With something as important as an argument over who has proprietary rights to the park bench, everything is clear, is on the surface, safe. In trivia there is no necessity for involvement: it is detached from such dangerous areas as the human heart.

The Zoo Story marks the beginning of what has been, to a large extent, Albee's continuing theme. In it, Jerry and Peter 'make contact' only in the play's melodramatic conclusion. Before that, there is the story of Jerry and the dog: for Jerry it is an all-important encounter, one in which he is able to see not only his own tragedy, but the tragedy of an entire generation; for Peter only a somewhat disturbing diversion, one to which he can close his mind. The dog, obviously intended as some form of universal symbol, yet touchingly believable, each day meets Jerry in the hall, then attacks him. One day, Jerry tells Peter, he reached his decision: 'First, I'll kill the dog with kindness, and if that doesn't work . . . I'll just kill him.' After an unsuccessful attempt to poison the animal, Jerry discovers that 'I had tried to love, and I had tried to kill, and both had been unsuccessful by themselves. . . . I hoped that the dog would understand'.

'Don't you see?' he asks Peter, 'a person has to have some way of dealing with SOMETHING. If not with people . . . SOMETHING.' And, after a long series of 'things', he concludes: '. . . with God who, I'm told, turned his back on the whole thing some time ago . . . with . . . someday, with people. People.'

Peter is seemingly uncomprehending throughout Jerry's entire long soliloquy. He reacts at the *proper* moments, of course: wincing at the proposed killing of the dog, but scoffing at the idea of 'contact' between Jerry and the dog. One really is not surprised at his 'I don't understand', for it has become obvious that Jerry expects too much when he seeks someone either to share or comprehend his own experience. Words alone cannot convey it. Peter and, by extension, most of modern man, is incapable perhaps, but more frequently unwilling, just as Jerry and the dog were ultimately unwilling: 'We regard each other with a mixture of sadness and suspicion', Jerry says, 'and then we feign indifference. We walk past each other safely; we have an understanding. . . . The dog and I have attained a compromise; more of a bargain, really. We neither love nor hurt because *we do not try* to reach each other.'

'I DON'T WANT TO HEAR ANY MORE', Peter

shouts. Indeed, he does not. For Jerry has come far too close to reaching him; has touched on a problem not merely his own, but that of every man. And so the return to trivia; to the parakeets and, eventually, to the bench dispute and the play's violent ending, wherein Jerry, forcing Peter into an open 'fight', asks him: 'Don't you have any idea, not even the slightest, what other people *need*?' His conclusion, excessively melodromatic though it is, is effectively reached when Jerry, having finally aroused Peter, forces a knife upon him, then impales himself on it.

In *The American Dream* (1961), Albee's *leit motif* assumes the form of comedy. Incisively satiric, bitingly ironic, the opening exchange between Mommy and Daddy—which occupies several minutes—is over so important, so earth-shaking, a point as the colour of Mommy's new hat; whether it is wheat-coloured or beige. It is the only level on which Mommy and Daddy attempt conversation; a conversation as empty, as meaningless, as the symbolic empty gilt picture frame that hangs over their sofa. It is not merely funny—perhaps not really funny at all. It is the tragedy of two human beings, the daily occupants of each other's world, who really exist without each other, yet attempt to love what they do not know. Albee has written that the names of the two characters are terms of 'empty affection and point up the pre-senility and vacuity of their characters'. It is this vacuity—and the vacuity of 'the American dream'—that absorbs him.

When a Mrs Barker comes into their home—she knows not exactly why, nor do they—she becomes part of Albee's world. A 'professional woman', she is involved in so many Good Works that she cannot keep them separated. Which of her committees, which of her Responsible Citizens Activities, has brought her there? She is the typical socialite, pursuing her works of 'charity' on alternate Mondays, Wednesdays and Fridays. And for what reason; for any motivation beyond filling in time? This is never verbally posed or answered, and perhaps it is just as well. Albee probably comes closest to it when he has Mommy inquire, 'Are you sure you're comfortable? Won't you take off your dress?' 'I don't mind if I do', Mrs Barker replies. One then wonders, amid the empty picture frames and the 'empty' boxes, whether, in the world of Albee's *American Dream*, anything is what it appears to be. The handsome young man who next comes to the apartment looking for work obviously is not. He describes himself: 'I no longer have the capacity to feel anything. I have no emotion; I have been drained; torn asunder . . . disemboweled. I have, now, only my person . . . my body . . . my face. . . . As I told you; I am incomplete. I can feel nothing. And so . . . here I am . . . as you see me. I am but this . . . what you see. And it will always be thus.'

Is this, then, the American Dream? Possessor of great surface values, yet empty inside, something sought after, yet, when found, unworthy of the seeking? Albee's Young Man, virile, handsome, seemingly the personification of the American ideal, yet a hollow man; illusory, a goal—a dream—which Albee seems to view as, not so much beyond attaining, but as not worth having once achieved. For the surface—the glitter, the chrome, whatever—is not the reality. Whatever else is said, however disarmingly or fantastically some of it is couched, there is always the American Dream—and it is always not exactly what it has appeared.

If there is any one thing that dominates both *The American Dream* and *The Zoo Story*, it is probably this: in a society seeking only the personal comfort, the status and the convenience of the material moment, human involvement, human sensitivities, must be ignored. Peter on the park bench denies Jerry's need; the Young Man's identical twin was once cruelly repudiated, spiritually and physically dismembered by 'Mommy' and 'Daddy'. All wish to inhabit their own private world; all wish, most of all, to avoid reaching that point at which they might begin to know, to experience, some share of another's agony.

In *Who's Afraid of Virginia Woolf?*, Albee brings that agony scorchingly to the surface. Nearly three and a half hours long, the play is a prolix indictment of contemporary society's frequent inability to distinguish illusion from reality, surface from essence. But it is more than that. The love–hate relationship of the middle-aged faculty couple, George and Martha, as it is hurled out in the presence of a younger couple, is a cascading torrent of expletives, vulgarity and imposed 'shock' effects (at least for its time). For all this—and its frequent transparency—*Virginia Woolf* is almost unquestionably the major theatrical experience provided by an American writer of Albee's generation. It shakes and excoriates, accuses and excuses, with an abandon and consistency seldom seen on recent American stages.

The 'Fun and Games' of Act 1 begin at 2 a.m. Nick and his young wife, Honey, have joined George and Martha for that they think will be a nightcap. What it turns into is an evening from which neither couple can emerge unchanged. In their liquor-sodden discontent, George and Martha cast aside the conventional banality of much modern conversation. Having long since discovered that to love is also to hurt, they carry their realization to its ultimate form. Martha is the daughter of the college president; George is the supposed faculty failure, the man for whom the bright future once envisioned has turned to the ashes of frustration. As they attack each other on this and other questions from the past, a present emerges. It is in this present that *Virginia Woolf* oversteps itself in its reliance upon a plot thread finally too flimsy to sustain the surface brilliance of its first two acts.

George and Martha have a son—or so they tell Nick and Honey. He is essential to their relationship, imperative to their need to rail each other for their respective failures with him. Yet, George warns her, 'Just don't start the bit, the bit about the kid'. In a sense, he is an echo of the Young Man in *The American Dream*. Frequent allusions to him provide much of the forward momentum in an otherwise largely plotless drama. When, in 'The Exorcism' of Act 3, it finally becomes apparent that he is, after all, illusory, the imaginary creature of their childless marriage, the play suffers from what borders on a *reductio ad absurdum*. In tying together the pieces, Albee has—as have so many before him—imposed a conclusion which is fundamentally artificial. It is more than merely artificial; it is melodrama tagged on to something inherently literal, tinsel as the appendage of realism. For George, in his revenge on Martha, his desire to win this 'game' they play, decides to 'kill' their imaginary son. Over this death of illusion he reads, in Latin, the prayers for the dead. Martha cries out that he cannot do it; cannot make this decision alone, but she pleads in vain. 'It will be better', George tells her. The illusions by and for which we live are fragile, Albee suggests, waiting only for the word by which they topple. That the word is not more frequently spoken is a testimony only to our civilized pretence, our power of self-deception. Were we to cut through them to a kind of ultimate and impossible honesty, foundations would alter, a world would be changed. Or, as George reminds Honey: 'When people can't abide things as they are, when they can't abide the

present, they do one of two things . . . either they turn to a
contemplation of the past as I have done, or they set
about to . . . alter the future. And when you want to
change something . . . you BANG! BANG! BANG!
BANG! BANG!'

In the flagellation and self-flagellation, the anguish
and peculiar kind of love of George and Martha, Albee
unleashes a verbal avalanche. Repetitive and excessive, it
is frequently also moving and startlingly evocative. There
remain, however, moments in which Albee's self-
indulgence causes one to pause. The achievement of
Virginia Woolf was a distinctly relative one. In saying, as
one critic did, that it towered 'over the common run of
contemporary plays', how much really had been said?

'Truth and illusion. Who knows the difference, eh,
toots?' George demands of young Nick. 'Truth and illusion, George; you don't know the difference', Martha insists to George. 'No,' he responds, 'but we must carry on
as though we did.' So they do, in their shared final agony
over the 'death' of the child they could not have, the child
George insists they had to 'kill'.

With *Tiny Alice* (1964) Albee continued to be controversial, but added an element of pretentiousness
and calculated obscurantism, a pseudo-*Cocktail Party*
atmosphere, that resulted in a deservedly brief
Broadway run.

A lawyer who once attended school with the Cardinal,
where they were ardent antagonists, arrives repre-
senting a client who wants to give $100 000 000 to the
Church 'now' and 'the same amount each year for the
next twenty'. She is 'overburdened with wealth'. It is one
of several 'bequests—arrangements' she (Miss Alice) is
making at the moment: to Protestants, to Jews, to
Catholics, to hospitals, to universities, to orchestras, to
'revolutions here and there'.

Brother Julian, the Cardinal's secretary, is to be sent to
take care of the 'odds and ends'. He is, the Cardinal says,
'an old friend of ours', a lay brother.

In Miss Alice's mansion is a 'huge doll's house model
of the building of which the present room is a part. It is as
tall as a man'. It is exact, 'even with tiny candlesticks on
the tables'. So exact that there is a model within the
model.

Miss Alice's lawyer has a dossier on Brother Julian, but
it has six 'blank' years, years when he was in his thirties,
and he declines to fill them in. When the lawyer is gone,

however, he admits to Butler, the butler, that 'I lost my faith. In God', and that he had put himself in a mental home.

When Julian first meets Miss Alice, she has a face that is 'that of a withered crone, her hair grey and white and matted; she is bent; she moves with two canes'. But he had been told that she was a *young* woman. Hers, however, is a disguise, a game. She tells Julian that Butler was once her lover, that the lawyer now is.

The bemused, utterly confused, Julian acknowledges: 'I imagined so many things, or . . . did so many things I thought I had imagined. The uncertainty . . . you know?' Miss Alice has what is perhaps the only feasible reply: 'Are you sure you're not describing what passes for sanity?'

Miss Alice decides he should perhaps 'move in' and thus be available to answer her questions.

As often happens, however, deliberate obscurantism becomes tedious. As Alice and the lawyer argue, the model catches fire. The chapel. But the actual chapel is on fire. When they succeed in extinguishing the fire in the house the one in the model goes out as well.

When Julian comes to stay in the house, he realizes he is being tested. Why? 'And why am I being tempted? By luxury, by ease, by . . . by content . . . by things I do not dare to discuss.' In time, he reveals his desire for martyrdom, is self-entranced when Alice suggests, 'Marry me'.

And marry they do, after further deliberate obscurantism. Then there occurs what is described as 'the ceremony of Alice', in which the 'great benefit to the Church' resulting from their marriage is alluded to. He is then told that he has married 'her', the Tiny Alice in the model. 'You are hers.' He insists he will return to the asylum, wondering whether *that* was when he was 'rational'.

Instead, the lawyer shoots him and, as they leave Julian goes through a long, long, *long* monologue in which he seems to equate Alice and God, the God who has apparently deserted him, but whose will he accepts.

Although Albee has claimed that the critics are to blame for imposing on *Tiny Alice* things he never intended, he is mistaken. It is a bad, and a pretentious play.

A Delicate Balance (1966), which received the Pulitzer Prize that many think should earlier have gone to *Virginia Woolf*, offers a marked and welcome change of pace. Like much of Pinter and the theatre of the absurd, of which Albee was at least marginally a member, it suggests a hidden, unnamed element of menace, disaster lurking just outside the door, perhaps just up the stairs.

Agnes and Tobias are a well-off couple in their fifties. Her sister, Claire, whom she has railed at earlier in the evening, returns to the living room in the play's opening scene to say: 'I apologize that my nature is such to bring out in you the full force of your brutality.' Tobias suggests that she attend meetings of Alcoholics Anonymous, but she responds with the glib sense of irony that characterizes her behaviour throughout the play: 'They were alcoholics, and I was not. . . . I was just a drunk. . . . They couldn't help it; I could, and wouldn't. . . . They were sick and I was merely . . . willful.'

Shortly thereafter, Harry and Edna, their best friends, appear quite unexpectedly. Why have they come? It seems they had been sitting at home and suddenly they 'got frightened'. There was seemingly nothing to cause it, says Harry, 'but we were very scared', and could not remain there, so they have come to visit Agnes and Tobias, who put them up in their daughter Julia's room.

Julia returns home the next day, yet another marriage—her fourth—on the rocks. Harry and Edna have remained upstairs all day. They appear briefly, with their coats, but it is only to announce they are going home to pick up their things and will return. When they do, they are clearly 'moving in'.

'Edna and Harry have come to us', Agnes tells Claire and Julia, 'dear friends, our very best, though there's a judgment to be made about that, I think—have come to us and brought the plague. Now, poor Tobias has sat up all night and wrestled with the moral problem', the problem of whether they shall be permitted to remain. When Harry comes downstairs, he asks Tobias 'Do you want us here?' but only moments later, he volunteers that, in Tobias's position, he would not let *them* stay. Tobias, however, insists they've 'cast [their] lot together, boy, we're friends'. He cannot keep up the facade, however; he wants them to leave and finally must acknowledge it, though still insisting they remain.

Edna, however, knows that it is all over. 'It's sad to come to the end of it', she says, 'nearly the end; so much more of it gone by . . . than left, and still not know—still not have learned . . . the boundaries, what we may not do

... not ask for fear of looking in a mirror. . . . It's sad to know you've gone through it all, or most of it, without . . . that . . . the only skin you've ever known . . . is your own—and that it's dry . . . and not warm.' And so they leave. Agnes, Claire and Tobias are left to themselves and, Agnes reflects, 'we'll all forget . . . quite soon'.

Every man, perhaps, is an island, with in the end only his own resources to draw upon, whether those resources include something known as the spiritual, a god, God—or nothing. Yet, he cannot avoid the process of life, with all it entails, or of death, even the small deaths that take place every day. It is the plague, the 'disease', that pursues him. In *A Delicate Balance*, an at times very funny, at others quite poignant, play, Albee alludes to all of this and makes it far more palpably believable than it was to be in either of his more recent works.

All Over (1971) is what is sometimes referred to as a 'difficult' play. A great man is dying. He is not otherwise identified; a politician perhaps; an artist or a financier. In the event, he is a celebrity. As the press and television crews lurk downstairs awaiting his death, others, too, maintain their vigil: The Wife, The Daughter, The Mistress, The Doctor, The Son, The Best Friend, The Nurse. Albee does not further identify them.

Albee is at his best when his characters are at their bitchiest. The Wife and The Mistress possess a degree of rapport. Both after all—the wife of fifty years and the mistress of twenty—love the man who is dying, bicker though they do over whether he should be cremated or buried, food for flames or food for worms. The children, middle-aged children, sulk about, failures and haters. Hated, too. Especially The Daughter, who periodically erupts in a vitriol, scorn and bitterness reminiscent of *Virginia Woolf*. The Best Friend and lawyer reflects—on his wife, on his former relations with the dying man's wife, on the things a deathwatch recalls—while the eighty-six-year-old Doctor and The Nurse occasionally leave their places beside the screened-off bed upstage to venture their own observations and memories.

Initially, they all speak in formalized cadences and heightened language, a dialogue that is both non-realistic and precise: 'This is what I have come to love you so little for: that you love yourself so little.' 'He said he thought not.' 'While I merely your wife of fifty years. . . .' 'Baleful as I suppose my gaze must have been to him.' Since this was Albee's twelfth play and he has written some of the most vibrant dialogue in the American theatre, it seems safe to assume the artificiality is intentional. It is not what Albee does best, and he does not do it well in *All Over*, though the language fortunately becomes somewhat more lifelike, if not really alive, as the play wears on.

The Wife talks of 'the little girl I was when he came to me' and The Mistress of her 'status' and her first love affair during a long-ago summer. The Daughter, who is incapable of love, lacerates her mother for her failure to do so; The Son, an emotional eunuch, finally becomes emotional when he details not some memory of his father's kindness or lack of it, but the unchanged contents of his bathroom.

So they continue through the play's two acts, haranguing each other, exhibiting their rancour and their venom, their sarcasm and their spleen. They seek themselves, but not within themselves. Virtually everything that emerges emerges in terms of their attempts to define themselves in relation to the dying man. It does not really work. We know no more of him when the play ends than we did in its first few moments and only marginally more of them.

'All we've *done* is think about ourselves. Ultimately', The Wife says as the play approaches its conclusion. There has been a great deal of talk and a great deal of surface emotion has been expended. There have been some completely riveting moments, but The Wife, The Mistress and all the rest are attempting to bring to life characters who are essentially the puppets of a playwright's vision, figures who move about speaking arias that refuse to sing, lines that refuse to resound in the vacuum of a deathwatch that ultimately has as little to say about living as about dying.

Seascape (1975) has been described, by the author, among others, as the 'life' part of a life/death play that began with *All Over*. Regrettably, life is one of the things it most obviously lacks.

A middle-aged couple by the names of Nancy and Charlie have been spending some time by the sea. 'Can't we just stay here forever?' she asks, for she loves the water as Charlie once did. As a boy, he wanted to live under the sea, wanted to be 'fishlike'. He used to go 'way down, and try to stay'. He would go in, 'take two stones, look up one final time at the sky . . . relax . . . begin to go down. . . . And one stops being an intruder, finally—just one more object come to the bottom, or living thing, part of the undulation and the silence. It was very good.'

Charlie hasn't, however, done it since he was seventeen and it has been 'too long' for him to go back again, as Nancy urges. He would rather 'remember'. He would rather do nothing. And that is precisely what they do for approximately thirty-five minutes of the first act: nothing but review their lives tediously and acrimoniously, though this acrimony has none of the acerbic bite and bitchy humour of *Virginia Woolf* and certainly none of the interest.

Just when tedium threatens to become numbness, two lizard-like creatures emerge from the sea. They are Sarah and Leslie and they too are apparently middle-aged (though telling a middle-aged lizard from a young lizard is clearly beyond my competence). At first, the two couples are afraid of each other, then gradually they begin to develop points of contact, are in turn aggressive, responsive, patronizing, curious. Charlie tells Nancy that what is happening is not real, that they are in fact dead from the liver paste they had at lunch. 'We ate the liver paste and we died.'

The two couples experience both harmony and conflict, things shared and things unknown to the other. What is one to make, for instance, of Nancy having had only three children, and taken care of them for twenty or more years, when Sarah has had seven hundred and abandoned them?

Albee, however, is more concerned with similarities than with differences. 'In the course of the play', he has commented in an interview, 'the evolutionary pattern is speeded up billions of revolutions.' Thus, it slowly evolves that Sarah and Leslie are, or have the potential to be, every bit as bigoted, every bit as middle-class in their values and behaviour, as Nancy and Charlie. They, however, aren't put off by blacks or 'foreigners', but by fish: 'There's too many of them; they're all over the place . . . moving in, taking over where you live . . . and they're stupid!'

Why had they come up from the sea, these two green-scaled creatures, who, at least, still enjoyed an innocence, a sense of wonder, long gone from the couple they have come upon? '*We* had changed', Sarah reveals, 'all of a sudden, everything . . . down there . . . was terribly . . . interesting, I suppose; but what did it have to do with *us* anymore?' So they came up from what Charlie refers to as the 'primordial soup, the glop'. What has been going on, he tells them, is 'called flux. And it's always going on; right now, to all of us.' And maybe, he admits, he envies them, 'down *there*, free from it all; down there with the beasts'.

Envy or no, Charlie causes Sarah to cry at the thought that Leslie will one day die, go away forever. It is an alien concept and Leslie attempts to choke him, for Sarah has never cried before.

'It's . . . rather dangerous . . . up here', Leslie concedes. 'Everywhere', returns Charlie. So they decide they will go back down again. It goes almost without saying, however, that they will not, cannot; the process must go on. 'You'll have to come back', advises Nancy, 'sooner or later. You don't have any choice.' And Sarah and Leslie recognize the truth of what she says, which prompts their anxiety. Nancy tells them she and Charlie could 'help'. At the curtain, Leslie has acceded: 'All right. Begin.'

As a course in very elementary Darwinism, *Seascape* just might have some value; as a play, it is pretentious, simplistic, verbose and banal. Albee prides himself on being a 'literary' writer, but is it literary or pretentious when Nancy advises: 'Charlie has decided that the wonders do not occur; that what we have not known does not exist; that what we cannot fathom cannot be; that the miracles, if you will, are bedtime stories; he has taken the leap of faith, from agnostic to atheist; the world is flat; the sun and the planets revolve about it, and don't row out too far or you'll fall off'?

As in *All Over*, the writing is presumed (by the author) to be poetic and resonant, profound, when in reality it is devoid of life and artificial, the producer of inertia. In *Seascape*, it would seem only to confirm what has become more and more evident with the passing years: that it is to such plays as *Tiny Alice*, *Malcolm*, *All Over* and *Seascape*, not the earlier, more vital and vibrant—even more profound—*Zoo Story* and *Virginia Woolf*, that one must look for the 'real Edward Albee'. It is a sad discovery to make.

6 Neil Simon

If the reports are accurate, and there's no reason to think they aren't, the most financially successful playwright in the history of the theatre—'ever'—is Neil Simon. Whether or not *Variety* had its figures precisely right, Simon has made millions, be they dollars or pounds. He is both better and worse than that suggests. He has, by now, as Walter Kerr says in *God on the Gymnasium Floor*, 'become not only rich but respectable'.

Simon arranges most of his own financing, owns his own theatre. His own hits go into his own house (at least most of the time), which makes for a pretty nice arrangement. Not even Shakespeare had it better. As Kerr notes: 'He opens a show, probably reads the reviews to see how his investment is going to do, then turns to his machine to tap, tap, tap out the next. He is, in effect, a nine-to-five fellow, daily and for all I know Sundays; in any case, there's always another play ready before the last has begun to slip from capacity. He *expects* himself to produce yearly, he treats his craft as a profession rather than an avocation or a mining expedition which may or may not strike gold, he is a steady and possibly compulsive worker.'

Neil Simon's career falls into two stages: the early, largely inconsequential, comedies and the more recent attempts at a comedy with serious undertones. The former have been hugely successful despite, or perhaps because of, their triviality and—I say this without condescension, for reasons that I trust will become obvious—do not really warrant extended discussion here. Simon himself has moved on from them. They were work entirely for the boulevarde of Broadway, for the theatre parties and the expense account crowd. They made it and established their author in a virtually invulnerable position. Since approximately 1970, however, Simon has sought to be taken more seriously, desires to be more 'meaningful', as he puts it. Which can be a mistake for a playwright whose forte remains the one-liner, the glib, easy gag, just as easily forgotten.

Barney Cashman, the hero of the 1969 play *Last of the Red Hot Lovers*, owns a seafood restaurant and a record of twenty-three years of uninterrupted fidelity to his wife. At forty-seven, he feels he's missed something and wants to have one, just one, extramarital fling, to *live*, before settling back into his routine of dreary but not really unhappy monogamy. Getting with the sexual revolution turns out to be considerably more difficult than he anticipated.

As would-be Casanovas go, Barney is hardly the type: rotund, balding, insecure, guilt-ridden, more than slightly hapless. But he does have his mother's apartment and convertible sofa for two hours a week while she's off doing hospital volunteer work, and it's there that he sets up the Great Assignation.

Actually, 'sets up' is just the term. In comes Barney, complete with galoshes which he carefully deposits on a newspaper just inside the door, an attache case containing the afternoon liquor supply and glasses, and an air of nervous determination that announces more clearly than any lines that this particular Don Juan isn't likely to make it.

If he doesn't, it's not for want of trying. The first attempt is with a cynical, sex-starved wife he's met at his restaurant (he didn't pay the bill). She may like sex—and preferably lots of it—but Barney apparently isn't her type after all; either that or she'd just like to get on with what she came for, while Barney, obviously only half-converted to the sexual revolution, would prefer to *get to know her* first.

It goes almost without saying that Barney doesn't make it the first time. Act 2 gives him another chance, this time with a kooky, paranoiac (and unsuccessful) pop singer who rooms with a Nazi lesbian who is 'a great vocal coach if you don't mind being whipped'. Apparently, Bobbi's sexual adventures have been of the more bizarre kind and Barney is doomed to a replay of Act 1's frustrations. This time, however, there are some compensations. It seems Bobbi's doctor has prescribed pot for her nerves, and she and Barney are well on the way to being stoned as the second act curtain descends.

Undaunted, Barney tries again, this time with his wife's best friend. It's worse than ever and all he gets for his effort is some melancholy philosophizing on the sorry state of the world and the even sorrier state of everyone in it ('My psychiatrist and I have decided that when we both think I'm ready, I'm going to get in my car and drive off the Verrazano Bridge'). 'Aren't you appalled by all the promiscuity you find everywhere?' she asks, stubbornly clutching her pocketbook in the face of his amorous advances. '*I* don't find it anywhere', he replies wistfully and, as the Act 3 curtain falls, his illicit encounters in ruins, he is calling his wife to the rescue, only to find she's not in the mood either.

Although such a brief description may make it sound rather slick—which, of course, it essentially is—*Last of the Red Hot Lovers* is also rather poignant in its way, a well-observed portrait of the middle-class, middle-aged American who feels he's missed *something* but isn't quite sure what (except that it *must* be mixed up with sex). It is well observed but not deeply observed. Simon's insights, like his humour, are usually of the more facile kind; his perceptions, like so many of his jokes, one-liners. You can do a lot with a one-liner, but the depth had better be there in the first place if you want to be taken as seriously as Neil Simon apparently does.

In *The Gingerbread Lady* (1971), Simon's flirtation with seriousness becomes a major affair.

Evy Meara is forty-three, a former cabaret singer and a nymphomaniac, with a fading apartment on Manhattan's West Side. There is a poster on the wall announcing a long-ago concert she gave in Carnegie Hall; the liner of her lone record album is conspicuously present in the record rack.

Evy is nowhere to be seen when the curtain rises. A middle-aged homosexual actor friend of hers darts about making preparations for her return. A Puerto Rican delivery boy arrives with some groceries and declines when he is told to charge them. The telephone company calls to say they are about to suspend service due to non-payment of bills. Clearly, Evy has seen better days.

Evy has spent ten weeks in a hospital trying to shake her long-time alcoholism. She has shed forty-two pounds and is determined that this time it will be different. That it won't be is fore-ordained: a three-act play requires her decline and fall.

That is part of the problem. Simon goes mechanically about setting up that fall. Evy's seventeen-year-old daughter, the product of a marriage that ended in divorce, arrives to stay with her. The homosexual actor goes off to yet another desperate audition, still attempting—but less and less successfully—to convince himself he *will* become a star. A forty-year-old friend, her face in her cosmetics case, comes on the scene, stridently trying to convince everyone that beauty and 'femininity' are all, cataloguing her conquests and almost frighteningly insecure. A guitar-playing former lover who deserted her in favour of an eighteen-year-old girl reappears, pleading to be taken back, and is sent away.

Evy, Jimmy, Toby and Lou are among the walking wounded. They rely upon each other for completion, for comfort, for the lie that wards off the truth. As her daughter tries desperately to help her mother reclaim her life—to succeed in that 'one more chance at this human being business'—the other three ensure that she will not. It is not that they will her downfall, rather that in their mutual weakness and dependence they lay out their own travails—a lost role, an impending divorce—and those travails lead Evy, who has already been sneaking a sherry or a beer on the side, into a complete fall off the wagon.

It is there that Simon left her until the negative response to the play's Boston tryout: drunk, deserted, in a darkened room, about to invite the delivery boy into bed. But audiences, critics and presumably Simon were unhappy. So the New York opening was postponed and the play extensively rewritten, to emerge with Evy determined to give it another try. Which, presumably, had more appeal to the theatre party ladies.

Unfortunately, the very ambivalence toward his material that would permit Simon so to alter his original intention infects the whole play. The wisecracks that cloak the anguish, the automatic ripostes that seek to hide the fear, in this case not only preclude dimension, they permit Simon the easy out. He does it all so easily—or seems to—and it is so easy *not* to take the final step, the one that would take him and the audience inside Evy, that would reveal what she is and why she is. Evy is lonely; Evy is frustrated; and Evy drinks; but Evy is a cliché without more personally revealing features, a woman with a past that made her what she is, but a past seldom more than hinted at. Whenever he seems on the brink of telling more, Simon pulls back. There is another one-liner, self-protection for the character, of course, but self-protection in another way for Neil Simon. Perhaps clowns should not play Hamlet after all.

Simon is the quintessential New York playwright, whether New York be geographical or a state of mind, and *The Prisoner of Second Avenue* (1971) is a prime example of why.

Mel Edison is forty-six years old and admits to his wife his fears that he is about to lose his advertising job. She suggests that if it happens they can move to Spain. There is, after all, nothing they'd miss about New York. But Mel isn't ready. 'I'm not through with my life yet. . . . I still have value, I still have worth.' To which she retorts: 'What kind of life is this? You live like some kind of a caged animal in a Second Avenue zoo that's too hot in one room, too cold in another, over-charged for a growth on the side of the building they call a terrace that can't support a cactus plant, let alone two human beings. Is this what you call a worthwhile life? Banging on walls and jiggling toilets?'

When he does lose the job, he returns home only to find they've been robbed. All he's been left with is a pair of khaki pants and his golf hat. But he's not about to need much more. 'He has no place to go and no desire to go there.' Indeed, he soon becomes convinced there is a plot, 'a plot to change the system. To destroy the status quo.' It's not only him that they are after. It's everyone. 'I'm out of work, that's my proof . . . They won't let me work!' Humouring him, Edna asks who is behind the plot. 'It is', he tells her, 'the human race! . . . It is the sudden, irrevocable, deterioration of the spirit of man.'

It goes almost without saying that Mel has had a breakdown. The pressure and stress have been too much for him especially in combination with the fact that Edna has returned to work. If this sounds more the stuff of tragedy or melodrama, one isn't bearing in mind the transmogrification of circumstances that can take place in Simon's typewriter. Though he does not succeed in making *The Prisoner of Second Avenue* fully successful either as comedy or as the something more he evidently intended, he does convey a sense of genuine compassion for his increasingly beleaguered couple and all too many moments of recognition for his also increasingly beleaguered audience.

With *The Sunshine Boys* (1972), Simon took another step in his progression toward seriousness. Willie Clark and Al Lewis, characters presumably based on the comedians Smith and Dale, spent forty-three years as vaudeville partners, 'The Sunshine Boys'. Then Al retired and became a stockbroker, breaking up the team once billed as 'the two kings of comedy'. Willie is living in a West Side hotel in semi—if distinctly unwilling—retirement, periodically visited and cared for by his young nephew–agent, Ben Silverman. As agent, Ben clearly has his problems. After all, what *can* you do for an actor who can't even crunch the potato chips in a potato-chip commercial?

One thing you can do is get him back together with his old partner as part of a television special on the golden age of comedy. Easier said than done, however, though Ben brings the two together all right, for a wary, insult-trading meeting and first rehearsal of an old sketch that has echoes of the fabled 'Dr Kronkite'. The two old men may not be overly fond of each other, but they do respect each other's talent. Asked by his nephew why he had worked with Al all those years, Willie responds with what from his angle was the essence of their relationship: 'As an actor, no one could touch him. As a human being, nobody wanted to touch him.'

One might think that eleven years apart must have mellowed them. Hardly at all. The first rehearsal in the TV studio breaks up in a quarrel. Al, it seems, has retained his annoying habits: He still insists on poking Willie with his index finger—'the toughest finger in show business'—and spraying him when he pronounces his 't's'. The agitation is too much for Willie. He has a heart attack.

He doesn't die, of course—this *is* a comedy—but his doctors tell him he must go to a home for old actors. And guess whom he's going to find there? Why his old friend–enemy Al, of course.

There are times when *The Sunshine Boys* is very funny. (Insisting he can 'do black'—play a Negro—Clark says: 'I did black in 1928. And when *I* did black you understood the words.') Others when it resorts to some of the creakiest of theatrical comedy clichés and tired jokes. (Someone they know has died: 'He died?' 'Last week.' 'Where?' 'In *Variety*.') Still others when Simon comes far closer to touching the heart, to creating characters of genuine poignance and inherent humour, than he has in the past. Yet, in the end, it leaves one a little cold.

The Good Doctor (1973) is only a footnote in Simon's career, though it was certainly a considerable departure for him. In it, he took nine of Chekhov's early stories and sketches and with a character known as 'The Writer' to

link them came up with something that was diluted
Chekhov and second-rate Simon. Although it had its occasional enjoyable moments, it was hardly sufficient to
make for a satisfying evening for fans of either the good
doctor, Chekhov, or 'Doc' Simon.

God's Favorite (1974) has to do with Job, otherwise
known as Joe Benjamin, who has made his millions in
cardboard boxes. He has great faith in and love for God,
however (or at least he so claims), which, in Simon's
hands, is bound to get him into trouble (and out). He
even goes so far as to pontificate: 'It is my belief that I have
been chosen . . . to test the faith and courage of man.'

Enter Sidney Lipton, the Lord's campy messenger,
('Important documents only. No packages'), complete
with a sweatshirt on which is emblazoned a large 'G'.
Sidney takes home $137 a week and, he admits, 'I hate this
job—I'd quit if I could only get a Carvel franchise near
Miami'. He has met God three times, 'twice on business,
once on a boat ride'. He's also met the Devil. 'He looks
just like Robert Redford—pink suit, that little mole on
his cheek!'

True, in a manner of speaking, to its source, *God's
Favorite* has Sidney inform Joe that Satan has bet God that
His favourite, Joe, will renounce him if the going gets
sufficiently rough. There follow tennis elbow and
psoriasis, beleaguerment by his hard-drinking, fast-
talking son, the devastation of Joe's Oyster Bay, Long
Island, mansion. To which the maid reacts, 'Well, I'll tell
you one thing: I ain't cleaning up *this* mess'. Needless to
say, the good guy triumphs in the end and recovers his
tycoondom. Explaining why he won't renounce his faith,
he tells his wife: 'I love God', only to have her respond,
'Why can't you just have a mistress like other men?'

That exchange suggests Simon's problem not just
with *God's Favorite* but with all too many of his earlier
plays. It is ever so clever, but very little of the humour
flows from the characters; the efforts at profundity
are shallow and unrewarding. Jokes all too often fall
back on quick references to brand names, TV shows and
the like. It is a cheap, easy and, regrettably, all too
frequently accepted, substitute for real humour.

Critics keep ruminating on what to make of Simon, unwilling, as he is unwilling, to take him for what he essentially is, far too eager to attribute a depth that at least
thus far simply does not exist, a depth he only aspires to.

He has written any number of plays—*The Odd Couple, Barefoot in the Park, The Star-Spangled Girl, Plaza Suite* and others—that at the time of performance seemed quite funny, though they do not seem nearly as much so on re-reading. That was not sufficient. If there is a moral, it is perhaps as simple as the old adage: you can't have it both ways (at least not in the contemporary theatre), rake in the dollars by the millions and solve even the minor problems of the world. As noted earlier, perhaps clowns should not attempt to play Hamlet after all. Then again, perhaps this particular clown—or Hamlet—may yet reach a point where he becomes something more than a relatively serious gag man, may take the leap and cease playing to the box office. As of this moment, the jury remains in recess, though it is hardly encouraging to note that Simon has recently pulled up stakes in New York and moved to Hollywood.

7 Sam Shepard

'I am truly American', says the young man in Sam Shepard's *Operation Sidewinder*. 'I was made in America. Born, bred and raised. I have American scars on my brain. Red, white and blue. I bleed American blood. I dream American dreams. I fuck American girls. I devour the planet. I'm an earth eater. No. I'm a lover of peace. A peace maker. A flower child, burned by the times.'

If ever a contemporary American playwright has written a more apt self-description than Sam Shepard did in these lines, I'd be hard-put to name him. For, although he has spent most of his time in London in recent years, Shepard is American to the core: its myths and images, its rhythms and its language, its hopes and its fears, its dreams and its nightmares. It is almost impossible to think of another writer who, rebelling at what he found, has at the same time been so much the embodiment of where he found it. Like so many others, he is in love with, indeed enthralled by, the America that was, appalled by what it seemed to be becoming (if not already had become).

Sam Shepard, who was born in Fort Madison, Illinois, in 1943 and raised in California, is a difficult playwright to write about—though there certainly hasn't been a lack of trying. He does not write about ideas, does not for the most part involve himself with causes, political or social. He is prolific almost to the point of excess (and I will discuss only a handful of his plays in detail; to do more would require almost a book in itself). Andy Warhol once said of his paintings: 'If you want to know everything about me, just look at the surface of my paintings, it's all there, there's nothing more.' Some of that was hyperbole, of course, but there was a large element of truth. To that extent, the same might be said of Sam Shepard. One can get far too involved in 'intellectual' analyses and wind up not seeing the proverbial forest for the proverbial trees, the essence, excitement and entertainment for the intellectual exercise.

In 1966, the *Village Voice* awarded Shepard an 'Obie', its Off Broadway award, for his three one-act plays *Chicago, Icarus's Mother* and *Red Cross*. They were, however, largely finger exercises, a playwright discovering he was a playwright. A number of plays in roughly the same category followed and were interspersed with more major efforts, the first two of which were *La Turista* and *Forensic and the Navigators*, both initially produced in 1967.

La Turista probably attracted more attention for banning reviews—a ban not universally honoured—than as a play. Which is fair enough, since it was an only intermittently interesting work. (Actually, it is two related one-acts, involving two of the same characters in altogether different times and places.)

In Act 1, Salem and Kent are tourists in a Mexican town. In the second act, which seems to have taken place before the first, they are in an American hotel room. In the first the 'cure' Kent is offered for his illness, *la turista*—diarrhoea, but also something more—comes from a witch doctor and his son, presiding over a ritual involving newly killed chickens. Kent dies, apparently of some form of sleeping sickness. Perhaps he has been on drugs. One is never sure with Shepard. Whatever the case, that it is an *American* ailment becomes even more obvious in the second act, where he winds up jumping through a wall, leaving the imprint of his outlined body. Regardless of the additional interpretations one wishes to inflict upon it, Elizabeth Hardwick is quite correct when she says in the introduction that Kent 'doesn't like to be awake'. Americans—and, increasingly, others—have been known to suffer from that disease. Shepard places one *in extremis*, but unfortunately without doing a very convincing or effective job of it.

The Unseen Hand (1969)—part science fiction, part caricature Western, part allegory—is Shepard very much into his own (mixed) bag, a sort of 'The Apocalypse Will Get You If You Don't Watch Out'. Blue Morphan, 'an ancient drunk going on 120 years thanks to modern medicine', wearing a scraggly buffalo coat and with bottle close at hand, has his colloquy with a decrepit '51 Chevrolet interrupted by a visitor from another galaxy. It's Willie the Space Freak, a quivering wreck who wants Blue to go with him to Nogoland to help set his people free from the tyrannical 'black magicians' who are subjugating them, the unseen forces who imprint the shape of a black hand on his forehead and squeeze down on it 'whenever his thoughts transcend' theirs.

It seems Blue and his two brothers, who were gunned down on the street a century or so ago—and are quickly 'summoned up' from their graves on Boot Hill—once made up a legendary western gang. Now, Willie pleads, they must accompany him to Nogoland to confront the High Commission. About this time a cheerleader from Azusa High School comes on the scene, pants dragging about his ankles, shouting obscenities through his megaphone, and manages to save his skin only by alerting them to the niceties of guerrilla warfare, which he seems to have learned by rote in school.

Shepard goes on like this for a while, taking pot-shots at many of the favourite American myths and realities. (Azusa, incidentally, stands for 'everything from A to Z in the USA'.) At times he resorts to clichés and banalities nearly on a par with those he indicts—'They have a revolution now and everything stays just like it was'; 'Why should you feel responsible for some species of hybrid from another galaxy?'—as Willie reminds the cowboy trio that 'freedom and revolution are inextricably bound up'. But he has the ability to create moments of such pure theatricality, such absurd humour—to go from taking himself much too seriously in one line to something completely bizarre in the next—that by the time Willie goes off proclaiming he has discovered he does not need their help after all, that he has found within himself all that is necessary to overthrow the Nogoland oppressors, it would be difficult indeed not to respond to his serio-pop comedy.

Forensic and the Navigators (revised, 1970) is considerably less effective. Two men are—or perhaps are not—involved in some sort of plot. As one hunches over a typewriter and tells the other to cool it, a girl comes on tossing a monumental flapjack. Then come a couple of 'exterminators', wielding their gas-spewing tools of the trade. Two characters go on a Rice Krispies trip, and everyone—or at least the audience—winds up rather thoroughly confused as the play ends with smoke cascading onto the stage, enveloping the actors, thence out into the audience. Shepard may know what he's going about, I surely don't.

Operation Sidewinder (1970) stars a computer in the form of a snake. Let loose in the desert by his Strangelove-like creator ('to help it discover its full potential'), the $2-billion computer wraps himself around a passing tourist and, while her husband is off getting help, proceeds to have a nicely erotic adventure. Before the husband can return, he's shot by the hippie hero–villain, who seems to be involved with a Black Panther plot to drug the water supply of the nearby Air Force base Sidewinder used to call home. (The machinations of that particular plot are far too complicated to go into. Fortunately, if a bit carelessly, Shepard appears to agree. It seems, however, to have something to do with getting all the pilots stoned so they'll fly off to Cuba.)

Eventually, a trio of Indians comes along and after decapitating Sidewinder, take his head, red eyes still flashing, off to the reservation. With that, the young conspirator reappears and, feeling badly in need of some stimulation, employs the body of the snake as a tourniquet so he can shoot up.

Sidewinder is that kind of play. It's also the kind of play in which a white car-hop at a drive-in restaurant tries, in a very funny scene, to radicalize three Panthers and the Air Force—and, for that matter, any other Establishment figures, black or white, Shepard happens on. About the only ones who emerge moderately unscathed are the Indians. It is left to one of them to relate an ancient myth concerning the severing of the head of a snake, after which 'all over the earth there was a mistrust and hatred', a hatred which abated with a rejoining of the head and body, symbolic of a coming together of the human race, only to be followed by yet another separation, which leads to cataclysm. (According to a programme note, there is a latter-day Hopi Indian prophecy which holds that the United States, apart from the Hopis and their homeland, 'will be destroyed, land and people, by atomic bombs and radioactivity'.)

Operation Sidewinder is at least partially a metaphor for that prophecy. It culminates in an Indian snake dance in which the young man and woman, two of those 'who take no part in the making of world division by ideology' (as the Hopis put it), join. They are survivors who are 'ready to resume life in another world, numbered among those of whatever colour who are 'all one, brothers'. But being brothers is not to be that easy. Troops appear looking for the head of the computer-snake, and, severing it again from its body, precipitate the new, presumably atomic, conflagration.

Shepard has the ability to create enormously effective moments, but in *Sidewinder* he does not succeed in bringing them together in a transcendent theatrical whole. Nor does he create characters with whom one can become in the least involved. The play is diffuse. It wanders about in search of itself. But it is alive. It is concerned with where we are. In writing about violence and technology, materialism, bureaucracy and moral blindness, Shepard would seem to be writing about nothing less than the disintegration of America.

Mad Dog Blues (1971) is a dream, a fantasy, a trip. Its characters are freaked-out refugees from the streets of New York, the mythology of America, the subculture of Hollywood. They go under such names as Kosmo (a former rock star), Yahoodi (a junkie), Marlene Dietrich, Mae West, Waco Texas, Paul Bunyon, Captain Kidd and Jesse James. They are, at least some of them, comic-strip figures whose denouement is not comic, questers who know not what they seek—their roots, perhaps. Like Shepard's play itself, they are bizarre, frightening and funny.

On their fantasy trips, Kosmo and Yahoodi travel to the North Woods and the jungle. Captain Kidd, Marlene and Yahoodi go in search of Kidd's treasure, pursued by Kosmo, Mae and Waco Texas. They are prepared to betray, even to kill, to obtain it. They are, however, 'gettin' fucking tired of apocalypses', and their treasure, like the gently satirized figures from our pop culture and mythology they encounter, is illusory. The treasure at the end of this treasure hunt is not gold, but bottle caps.

There's seldom much point in attempting to figure out what Sam Shepard 'means'. Although *Mad Dog Blues* probably could be approached schematically and its metaphors pursued to exhaustion, it would be a mistake to attempt it. Here, as elsewhere, Shepard is a creator of *theatre*, not of some self-conscious metaphysic. His characters and his ideas exist on the stage, where they do so with enormous verve, humour and, surprisingly, poignance. They are there to respond to, not to 'understand' —save, perhaps, on some other level of consciousness.

Back Bog Beast Bait (1971), another of Shepard's West-oriented plays, has to do with a couple of gunmen whom Maria has brought in to defend her against the devouring beast, Tarpin, 'the pig beast', who already has claimed her husband and her daughter. Slim tells Shadow: 'That Tarpin beast means to annihilate the human race. . . . This woman and her baby boy and her unborn in her belly are the last living things in this neck of the woods. And once it finishes with its dirty work here it's gonna move on.'

He is right. The beast returns and kills Maria's son. But Shepard is not into any form of intellectual who-dunnit. He is involved with something far closer to what we are all involved with. There is a speech by Slim that not only embodies it but may embody the essence of Shepard. He says:

'I move outside myself. It must have been another time. That's it! Another time! This is wrong! I'm not here at all. It was honky tonks and bathtub gin! Railroad men and mule skinners! That was it! This is all wrong! I'm out of my depth. The hands reach for something else now! There's a different craving! A new hunger! I'm starving to death and fat on buffalo meat! What is it a man cries for when nothing fits? No sense to the music? A new kind of music! A new kind of dance!'

If that is not Sam Shepard, and America, it would be difficult indeed to say what is. Regrettably, *Back Bog* itself is one of Shepard's weaker recent plays.

In *Cowboy Mouth* (1971), Cavale tells Slim: 'People want a street angel. They want a saint but with a cowboy mouth. Somebody to get off on when they can't get off on themselves. I think that's what Mick Jagger is trying to do . . . what Bob Dylan seemed to be for a while. A sort of god in our image . . . ya know? . . . We're earthy people and the old saints just don't make it and the old God is just too far away. He don't represent our pain no more. . . . It's like . . . the rock-n'-roll star in his highest state of grace will be the new saviour . . . rocking to Bethlehem to be born.'

Slim, however, is not cut out for the role, nor does he aspire to it. There is a plenitude of colourful, evocative writing in *Cowboy Mouth*, but it is really little beyond another finger exercise for Shepard.

The Tooth of Crime (1973) is considerably more than

that, in fact it is one of Shepard's most powerful plays so far.

Hoss, rock star and apparently sometime 'killer', is close to the top. But quite a few years have passed; he is becoming, perhaps already is, out of touch. Others are on the rise. It is, as it always has been, a time when, 'Everybody's doin' time for everybody else's crime. . . . All the heroes is dyin'.'

It is a time ripe for Crow, a gypsy, playing outside the 'code'. He crystallizes things, constitutes the threat, embodies the mores that created him. He is willing to take Hoss on, to take him on on his own turf.

They meet, but not with the weapons Hoss, the old marker, would prefer; rather, with Crow's weapon, style. It will be a fight to the death, for there isn't room for the two of them. One world must replace another and in its turn be replaced yet again.

Crow is going to 'win'. It's the way things are and we know it from the beginning, but Hoss won't go down without a fight. They battle—verbally, putting each other down. Hoss's girl re-enacts her presumably initial seduction by him, a black leather jacket serving as a substitute for the missing, now fantasized, body of her lover.

Crow does, of course, win. Hoss, failing and faded, must either be killed or kill himself. He is, or is about to become, a fallen idol. America has no time, no time at all, for fallen idols.

The Tooth of Crime is at times absolutely stunning in its verbal dexterity, its ability to employ language. There is no young American playwright who can touch Shepard in this. His idiom is a very hyped-up idiom of and for America. He rejects his country and is inextricably drawn to it; he writes of cowboys and used cars; of stars and star-gazers, and it is only when he seeks to get away from a language and an imagery that come so naturally to him, when he seeks for some more 'mid-Atlantic' language as he has in one or two recent plays, that he loses the distinct and individualistic qualities that make his work at times so exhilarating.

Geography of a Horse Dreamer, first produced at London's Royal Court Theatre in 1974, displays some of this loss.

Cody is from Wyoming, a young man whose distinction lies in the fact that he has a genius, a gift, for predicting the outcome of horse races. Now that gift has failed him and, with two thugs for the syndicate that has been exploiting him, he is holed up in a sleazy hotel room, manacled to the bed, trying to dream new winners.

But it's no good. All he gets is 'a fuzzy picture'. All he can come up with are champions from an earlier time: Silky Sullivan in the seventh, Native Dancer in the eighth. Cody tries to explain his problem to the two men: 'It's very delicate work, dreaming a winner. . . . It takes certain special conditions. A certain emotional environment.'

Santee and Beaujo, the two syndicate henchmen, however, live in another world, the world of the quick track payoff. If 'Mr Sensitive', 'Mr Artistic Cowboy', as they call him, can't produce a prediction on a winner he is of no use to them. Although they have been living off him, are unable to function without him, they have only scorn and impatience for his present state. They won't even let him out of the hotel room, won't even tell him where he is. Or, as he says: 'I'm dreaming American horses but we're probably in Morocco somewhere. It don't make sense. I gotta know where we are so I can adjust. I've lost track of everything. I need some landmarks.' He is, in other words, like a very large part of his country.

Suddenly, however, he makes the great switchover: he can predict the outcome of dog races—in an Irish accent. He—and they—can win again. But it is a winning that leads to madness. Confronted with the boss, Fingers, and the Doctor, he loses contact with reality. 'The mind is a very mysterious thing, ya' know', says Beaujo. Cody, in fact, changes from man to animal, turning into one of the dogs he thinks—dreams—he has been observing: 'I kept crying for trap one. Over and over again I asked for trap one. I could've won from the inside!'

The Doctor decides on a transplant, for he collects 'dreamers' bones' from the backs of their necks. Just as he has cut into Cody to remove his, Cody's two brothers, Jasper and Jason, burst in, come to return him to his native Wyoming, but not before killing the Doctor, Beaujo and Santee with their shotguns. The Doctor is not be be 'eternally linked to the dreamer's magic' after all. Cody will at least get to go back to the clear air, the purity, he once knew.

Shepard subtitles *The Geography of a Horsedreamer* a

'mystery play'. If America is a mystery, perhaps an expatriate like Shepard is in the best position to solve it, at least to fathom some of the contradictions that remain so elusive to his compatriots at home. As he is leaving, Cody speaks of: 'This day. Sacred. I was walking in my dream. A great circle. I was walking and I stopped. Even after the smoke cleared I couldn't see my home. Not even a familiar rock. You could tell me it was anywhere and I'd believe ya'. You could tell me it was any old where.'

In Shepard's case, the farther he has got from his roots, as in *Horsedreamer* and *Action* (1974), the more he has lost touch with their resonances. For Shepard, the internal landscape of the horsedreamer apparently is not enough. Though he may continue to use his cowboy names—his Cody, Slim and Cheyenne, Cisco, Sycamore and Blue—and his distinctly American mythology, his most recent plays seem to have lost something of their inner energy, their, at times, almost magical reflection of the things that gave them birth. In *Action*, Jeep, feeling trapped, observes: 'Everything disappeared. I had no idea of what the world was. I had no idea how I got there or why or who did it. I had no reference for this. . . .' It may be that Shepard, too, is losing his reference, his feeling for the distinctly American milieu and idiom that provided him with so much of his dynamism. Jeep also says, 'I'm looking forward to my life. . . . I'm looking forward to uh—me.' It would be a mistake for anyone looking forward to the future of the English-speaking theatre not also to be looking forward to what Sam Shepard will find, the decline in his most recent plays notwithstanding.

8 David Rabe

David Rabe is in his mid-thirties, the only one of his generation, the second 'postwar generation' of emerged or emergent American playwrights, to have served in Vietnam. Like his country, he has not yet truly got over it. His most successful plays deal with it directly; his efforts to move on betray the same halting steps as did those of his country as it entered the last quarter of the twentieth century. That said, he is nonetheless the most significant American playwright to appear since Albee; Sam Shepard, who remains distinctly American despite his recent years having been spent in London, being the only major contender.

The Basic Training of Pavlo Hummel (1971) remains the best play yet spawned by the Vietnam War (which, admittedly, is not saying much since most of them have been so relentlessly polemical and one-dimensional that one's only reaction could be political, not artistic).

Rabe's play is anything but one-dimensional. Indeed, its major failing is that the playwright has attempted so many layers that the focus is at times diffused. Overall, however, it is an impressive and effective work. Then, too, Rabe has a sense of humour, which helps enormously.

Pavlo Hummel's terrain is familiar. In the opening scene, a hand grenade thrown by a jealous and angry sergeant ends Pavlo's life on the floor of a Saigon whorehouse. The remainder of the play is a flashback in which Pavlo, a confused and quirky kid, quixotic and eager to please, anxious to find his manhood, moves through basic training, lying to his fellow trainees about his exploits as a car thief, anxiously preparing for the proficiency test that comes at the end of his eight weeks of training, gung-ho about being a soldier, yet anything but a brutal, hard-nosed killer.

First Sergeant Tower bullies, exhorts and cajoles his rookies from a high platform, putting them through their drills, extolling the merits of duty–honour–country. Another uniformed figure, a black officer named Ardell, moves in and out of Pavlo's life, adviser and observer, conscience and goad, ironically telling the anything but typical Pavlo, 'You black inside. I look at you. You black on the inside'. He is, however, the weakest element in the play, never fully integrated or defined.

Donning his dress uniform and sunglasses, Pavlo takes on a new and cocky identity. 'You so pretty, baby, you gonna make 'em cry', Ardell tells him. 'You tell me you name, you pretty baby!' Pavlo springs to attention: 'PAVLO MOTHERHUMPIN' HUMMEL!' In gear, he is the figure of his fantasies: tough, sure of himself, the potent lover.

In Vietnam after a brief furlough, he rebels at being made a medic. Pavlo wants to fight—to kill—but with an odd and naive charm. He gets his wish and is thrice wounded. All the while, death goes on around him: Vietnamese peasants are shot (and, surprisingly, it turns out that they *are* Vietcong). A soldier who lies downstage, crying out in agony as his life ebbs away from a stomach wound, is finished off by two darting, black-garbed VC. An older soldier, both legs and one arm amputated after a landmine explosion, lies in his hospital bed beseeching visitors to kill him: 'Some guys have a stump. I am a stump.'

Eventually, Pavlo dies in the whorehouse, a pointless death in a long since pointless war. He has, perhaps, achieved a partial self-identity, but the what or the why of that identity is never really clear. It is as if Rabe himself had not quite decided. Or perhaps that is the point. Perhaps the Pavlo of Act 1 and the Pavlo of Act 2 are really very much the same, neither hero nor villain, neither a bad guy nor a good guy, but a lonely, confused and infinitely fallible man.

If the ambiguity of Pavlo is at times disturbing, there is a reverse of the coin that gives the play much of its impact and dimension. Rabe does not make anything—apart from the hell of war—*that* black and white. He avoids both easy sentimentality and facile point-scoring. His Vietcong are no more heroic than his Americans (which, at a certain point, came to seem almost refreshing). It is war itself that becomes the horror story, a tragi-comic nightmare in which no one really can win, in which casual inhumanity is as likely to be found in the black pyjamas of the Vietcong as in GI battle dress. It is that—the refusal to be simplistic—together with Rabe's ability to create pungent and evocative, and believable, dialogue and unstereotyped characters that lifts *Pavlo Hummel* above such agit-prop exercises as Megan Terry's *Viet Rock* and George Tabori's *Pinkville*, two of the other better-known Vietnam War plays.

Rabe's erratically fascinating *Sticks and Bones* (1971) is a sequel to *Pavlo Hummel,* though it contains none of the same characters.

It is autumn of 1968 and the family of a young soldier has just learned that he is about to return home from Vietnam. They are Middle America personified: concerned with their possessions, the wife an avid church-goer, the husband at least mildly frustrated with the course his life has taken, the son a guitar-toting extrovert with sex—and fudge—on his mind and a continuing 'Hi, Mom! Hi, Dad!' on his lips. In other words, not what anyone would call 'bad' people, perhaps only painfully average in their desire for security, happiness and continuity.

Sticks and Bones displays many of the same concerns as *Pavlo Hummel*, especially with Vietnam (and by extension any other war), what it has done to the participants and what it reflects of their values and sensibilities. Unlike *Pavlo*, its focus is uncertain at times, its style a not quite satisfactory mixture of menace and melodrama, satirized soap opera, fantasy and savage insistence.

David's appearance in their home shatters the complacency, destroys the equilibrium, of his family (appropriately, if a bit too obviously, named Ozzie, Harriet and Rick after the celebrated TV family the Nelsons). For David is not only blind, he is embittered. Not over his blindness, but over what he *has* seen and especially over what he has left behind: a girl he loved and wanted to bring back home with him, but who is there only in his dreams and fantasies. The family he finds means nothing to him, in fact epitomizes all he has come to hate.

His is a bitterness and a scorn that the family itself cannot comprehend—and it is one of the play's weaknesses that Rabe never really makes it fully rational or comprehensible to the audience either. If they can see only that David is 'troubled, deeply troubled'—as his mother tells a priest she calls upon for advice—the audience, too, is offered only fragments of the reasons and an absent core.

Running parallel to David's torment is his father's. It is quieter—a quiet desperation, if you will—and he has been able to suppress it until now, to live with the fact that he 'grew too old too quickly' and that his future will never be what he dreamt of in a long bygone past.

David will not permit him to submerge his wounds any longer, not any more than he will let his well-meaning if rather vapid mother attempt to talk to him or the hearty priest (with his copy of *Psychology Today*) to counsel him. His mother he accosts with his cane; the priest he strikes and drives off with it.

All the while, a white-gowned Vietnamese girl moves back and forth from upstairs bedroom to living room: the 'yellow whore' of his parents' racist fears and accusations, the girl he loved and left behind.

In the end, David can only die, commit his symbolic suicide, if things are to 'get back to the regular way'. It is a scene of almost Feifferesque dimensions in its combination of horror, humour and banality. But, says one of his family, David is not going to die, 'only going to nearly die'. With that 'death' presumably will come a full return of the moral blindness David has attempted to deny them.

If the symbolism of *Sticks and Bones* is at times too heavy-handed, the material not entirely in control, the play, which won the New York Drama Critics Circle Award, does communicate an at times chilling sense of moral outrage. Perhaps it is merely ungrateful to ask of it something more.

The Orphan (1973), the third play in Rabe's Vietnam trilogy, is both more ambitious and vastly more flawed than the earlier plays, dense in its imagery and symbolism, but without the intensity and cohesiveness of those works.

Rabe seeks to interweave the Greek myth of *The Oresteia*, violence at home (in the form of the Charles Manson 'family') and at Mylai, hallucinogenic drugs and the scientific information explosion of today. Not surprisingly, it turns out something of a hotchpotch.

The diffusion of image and impact that results seems in part intentional, if misguided. Some characters appear in modern dress (Agamemnon, for instance, as a general). The two aspects of Clytemnestra, one tortured and essentially sympathetic, the other cruel and vengeful, are played by two actresses, something that does not so much work against the play as seem entirely unnecessary, a belabouring of the obvious. Orestes, Apollo and others occasionally switch into a rock number and the former is given a red telephone through which to speak with Electra. A 'speaker' moves about the stage with a hand mike, offering a scientific/ psychological commentary.

Meanwhile, members of the Manson family lounge about and one explains the rationale for their murders. Murder, violence, can be, always have been, rationalized by men and nations, Rabe suggests. Experts, whether they prophesy from a bird's entrails or computer input, are the same and trusted with the same blind faith in every age. And with somewhat similar results.

In his programme note, Rabe wrote that he found in Orestes 'a thematic brother of the peace movement', and went on to draw a parallel between his reaction to the murder (i.e., abandonment) of Agamemnon (father/'the ideals and principles of the land') by Aegisthus and Clytemnestra (mother/'the land itself') and the peace movement's call for revolution because the land had abandoned its ideals.

Like most such explanations after the fact, this one seems artificial and unconvincing in terms of what actually takes place on stage. If the drawing of elaborate parallels is necessary, then, somewhere along the line, the play itself has clearly gone amiss. Aeschylus' exploration of the moral background of the Trojan War, delivered by the Chorus of Argive elders in *Agamemnon*, remains far more telling, even for the audience of today.

There is a murkiness, an intellectual clutter, to *The Orphan*. It is almost as if Rabe, in his frustration and anger, felt the need to deal in apocalyptic, all-encompassing terms. The resulting play, with its divergent factors and styles, becomes too fragmented, too without narrative force, either to involve or affect the audience.

Despite these flaws, *The Orphan* is in no sense to be discounted with that most patronizing of terms, 'an interesting failure'. It does fail, but its failure is the consequence of aspirations on a scale so much broader and deeper than those of virtually any other American playwright writing today that the American theatre has a considerable stake in Rabe's discovering *why*. Especially since *In the Boom Boom Room* has certain of the same difficulties.

Boom Boom Room (1973, revised 1974) has as its central character a Philadelphia go-go dancer named Chrissy who is trying 'to get some goddam order in my stupid life', and right there we have one of the play's major problems, one only marginally rectified in the revised version of the play. For, if an audience is to spend three hours with a character, she had better be interesting, and Chrissy, appealing and sympathetic in her way, is not. Instead, she is yet another in a long line of Marilyn Monroe-like figures, wanting desperately to be taken seriously, unable to articulate her loneliness, unable to fulfill her needs. She aspires to what she does not have without knowing why or even what it is. Her ambition: to become a famous topless star in New York.

'I been gettin' a lotta important thoughts lately, see', she tells her mother, ' 'cause I'm all crammed with stuff I never knew enough to think about before, but it's all me.' Or, speaking of her dreams, her vision of her future career: 'I'm gonna be golden. I gotta be golden. I wanna be golden.'

This is Chrissy's level of articulation and, if it is also that of doubtless innumerable 'real-life' people, it remains insufficient in the theatre, especially for a character who is asked to carry almost the entire burden of the play.

Chrissy is surrounded by a pretty shallow and un-savoury lot, from a father who spiked her milk with vodka and apparently assaulted her sexually when she was a child to a bisexual dance captain who would like to have a lesbian affair with her. The men in her life range from Al, the bigoted stud who brutalizes her, to a homosexual who sells his sperm to a sperm bank. As for her mother, she made her 'nearly an abortion'.

Chrissy has survived them all, along with various others, but only that. At the conclusion, she is being introduced by the M.C. of a New York discotheque. Ob-viously, Rabe has no intention of the audience thinking Chrissy has 'made it', had her dream come true—or even found out what it really was.

Boom Boom Room, Rabe's fourth play, is his first not about the Vietnam War, and it contains some fine and highly theatrical writing and some moments of power and humour. But they are not sufficient to lift it above tedium more than briefly. Neither Chrissy nor any of those who glance off her life show any appreciable development and the play is wordy, diffuse and ill-focused. Rabe's obvious, at times touching, compassion for Chrissy and for the whole stratum of human beings she symbolizes notwithstanding, she remains insufficiently interesting and the play insufficiently dynamic to succeed.

Despite the failure of *In the Boom Boom Room* and of the earlier *The Orphan*, Rabe, so unlike Shepard, remains, with him, one of the most fascinating playwrights of his generation, a generation still only beginning to discover itself. He can write, write in ways that are searing, a style that is capable of poetry, a form that provides extraordinarily vivid and dynamic confrontations. He is far too talented to go down on the records only as a prisoner of Vietnam and it requires little critical prescience to suggest that he will not.

9 Newer Voices

Off-Off Broadway began in roughly 1960. It was, as Ellen Stewart, the guiding spirit of the LaMama Experimental Theatre Club, likes to say as she rings the cowbell at the beginning of each performance, a theatre 'dedicated to the playwright and all aspects of the theatre'. Yet, although it has produced literally thousands of plays by hundreds of playwrights, it has, over the course of some fifteen years, come up with relatively few playwrights of distinction. The reasons for this are not as obscure as they might at first seem. They have to do primarily with standards, secondarily with elitism, the cult and the clique.

With a few exceptions—notably Sam Shepard and Lanford Wilson, with perhaps Terrence McNally and Jean-Claude van Itallie added—most of the first generation of off-Off Broadway writers have failed to develop either in insights or technique. Intentionally or otherwise, they have generally continued to write for the small band of off-Off Broadway followers and practitioners whose theatrical bible is the *Village Voice*. On occasion, they have done some very exciting things; far more often they have been self-indulgent and hence self-defeating. Even so, the American theatre would be a pretty dull place without them.

Apart from Shepard, van Itallie, who was born in Belgium in 1936 and brought to the United States by his family in 1940, is probably the most interesting, certainly the most diversified, of the lot. *America Hurrah* (1966), three one-acts dealing with the 'illusion of eternal safety and universal happiness' as a cloak for underlying violence in three areas of American life—work (*Interview*), entertainment (*TV*) and travel (*Motel*)—is his best-known work, principally because many of his later efforts have been arrived at in collaboration with the Open Theatre rather than as the product of a single writer's intelligence and imagination. *America Hurrah*'s three plays are small satiric gems, as pertinent today as when they were produced.

Van Itallie has said that he does not so much seek to write a play as to 'construct a ceremony'. At various times in the past, he has indicated a certain distrust of words, although he remains one of the most gifted of their purveyors in the English-speaking theatre. More recently, however, he has provided a new English version of Chekhov's *The Seagull* (1975), so it may well be that he is returning to the more verbal fold.

The Serpent, although nominally a collaborative work, for which van Itallie provided the 'words and structure', remains his most impressive play thus far. It has its origins in Genesis and the Fall and its meaning in the present. In it, unlike some future collaborative offerings of the Open Theatre, there is no attempt at avant garde obfuscation. Indeed, many of the lines are taken directly or adapted from the Old Testament.

To a suprising extent, *The Serpent* meets van Itallie's goal of 'a ceremony', operating throughout in terms of myth and ritual, employing forms and techniques that invite a communal reaction to repressed personal emotions and to shared and traumatic recent American history. Lines are often chanted and there is frequent contrapuntal delivery, rhythmic choral humming, carefully formalized movement and frequent repetition in the manner of religious ceremonies or litanies. As in a religious ceremony, the lines and the action interact, complementing and clarifying each other to achieve their meaning and effect.

There are several quite extraordinary scenes in *The Serpent*, the first of which occurs even before the cast has begun to re-create the events in the Garden of Eden. Four actors assume positions similar to those of the Kennedys and the others in the car on that afternoon in Dallas, then begin to re-enact the moments so familiar from the countless film replays of the assassination. They smile, they wave; a 'crowd' in the background moves from side to side to simulate the effect of the car's movement. The President is shot, then the Governor. The President falls against his wife; her realization begins, and her horror. She starts to crawl out on what would be the rear of the car and to extend her hand. It is all done to a shouted twelve-count, as if in slow-motion. Then it is repeated, the 'film' played backwards; random numbers are called out out of sequence and their positions assumed.

Another figure appears and begins softly to speak lines reminiscent of Dr Martin Luther King's 'I have a dream' speech. He is shot. Yet another comes forward. He flicks a shock of hair back from his forehead, grins a little shyly, shakes hands in campaign style—and is shot. The three assassinations are repeated, begin to overlap, gaining in speed and intensity, as the crowd ritualistically repeats: 'I was not involved ... I am not a violent man./I am very sorry, still/I stay alive.'

It is the next scene, 'The Garden', that is the most fully realized in terms of combining elements of ritual, improvisation and audience involvement. As a chorus intones, 'I've lost the beginning ... I'm in the middle,/Knowing neither the end/Nor the beginning', actors begin to form the creatures in the Garden of Eden. The serpent emerges, formed by five actors—writhing, hissing, hands, legs and arms moving, tongues flicking. The effect is quite remarkable. The serpent tempts Eve, with first one actor then another speaking, holding out the apple, challenging her to eat. She succumbs and urges Adam to join her. The ecstatic serpent separates and two large cartons of apples are emptied on to the floor, then handed and tossed to the audience.

God's curses on mankind, strikingly adapted by van Itallie, and the murder of Abel by his brother Cain follow. Although somewhat overextended, this is probably the play's most effective scene, certainly its most originally conceived, with its leit motif: 'And it occurred to Cain/To kill his brother./But it did not occur to Cain/That killing his brother/Would cause his brother's death./For Cain did not know how to kill/And he struck at his brother./And broke each of his brother's bones in turn/And this was the first murder.'

In succeeding scenes, Man discovers sex, as the Old Testament 'begats' are intoned, and Man discovers death. It is all part of a path undertaken when his first decision, his first choice, was made. If Man has created God in his own image, created Him because he felt some need for limits or definition, he has created Him nonetheless. For better of for worse, he must live with Him and with the fears, shame and sense of sin that accompany it all. In time, the cast moves off into the audience singing 'Moonlight Bay'.

Although there are times when both van Itallie's and the 'collaborative' invention wane and any number where the scenes are overly protracted, *The Serpent*, at least as presented by the now regrettably defunct Open Theatre, possessed greater sustained impact, more arresting images, than virtually any other example of experimental theatre of the period. It recognized the necessity to blend word and image, to speak to the audience's intellect and sensibility as well as to its emotions and to do everything to a unified purpose.

Sadly, *Nightwalk* (1973), described as 'a collective work created by the Open Theatre', with three 'contributing writers', van Itallie, Sam Shepard and Megan Terry, fell far short of it.

Two creatures—birds, presumably, though other speculation has been offered—begin a nightwalk through our lives. They encounter a succession of American stereotypes, most of them rolled on on what look to be large garment racks. At times, a figure exists in isolation, at others, merges into a group or satirized situation. Much of it is only vaguely comprehensible. The speech was deliberately muffled or garbled—there is no published text—with only occasional words emerging with clarity.

The high point, which wasn't very, was a dinner party in which the actors parody human speech and mores, presumably in an effort to illustrate their hypocrisy and vacuity. What *Nightwalk* in fact illustrated was the consequences of a work with an intellectual vacuum at the core, little more than one very unoriginal idea in its head (or three heads). It attempted to substitute movement, mime, gymnastics, inarticulate sounds, for meaning and commentary and, in the absence of genuine development, deteriorated into tedium. Abandoning language in search of a new language that would say 'more', it made the mistake of equating *more* with *different*. It would be interesting to speculate on whether its relative failure was in any way responsible for van Itallie's subsequent return to more verbal theatre.

Mystery Play (1973) evolved from a section of an earlier play, *The King of the United States*, which, in revised form, was resurrected in 1974. It was tedious, only sporadically funny and overly portentous in its calculated obscurantism.

Briefly, it is set at a cocktail party in Washington. A senator and his wife preside and in attendance are their son Edward (a bisexual played by two actors), a Harvard professor, a high-class call girl, a butler and a woman mystery writer. At various moments the mystery writer steps outside the play to tell the characters and the audience what is about to happen. What is about to happen is that each will be murdered: one with a poisoned coffee, a second with a knife, a third blown up, another with a poisoned African ruby ring—and so on.

It is satirized mystery rather than actual mystery, and whodunnit doesn't really matter. Van Itallie seemed to have in mind some political point-scoring to go with his farce, but it wound up not mattering. I suspect that the only one who *may* conceivably have known what he was about was the playwright. He should have left the audience something of a clue.

Only a word about van Itallie's English version of *The Seagull*: It was a good, at least workman-like, product. It had the possibility of playing considerably better than its production allowed. Certainly, it exhibited van Itallie's facility with *language*, with words, even though he has spent so much time with a company that increasingly drew away from words. It is not without interest—in fact it may be the most interesting thing to have happened in the American theatre in a good many years—that Jean-Claude van Itallie and Joseph Chaikin, after years of trying to get away from words, from so-called verbal theatre, wound up, early in 1975, collaborating on a production of *The Seagull*. It was a production in many ways flawed, but, the dangerous nature of predictions notwithstanding, I would hazard to suggest that, some five or ten years from now, that single development will have portended something quite substantial in terms of the evolution of the American theatre.

Lanford Wilson, who was born in Lebanon, Missouri, in 1938, is one of the relative handful of off-Off Broadway playwrights who has 'made' it. Not uncharacteristically, he did not make it with his best play, *The Madness of Lady Bright*, an early off-Off Broadway triumph at the legendary Caffe Cino in 1964, but with *The Hot L Baltimore* (1973), a good, well-crafted, sporadically moving, but entirely conventional work, first produced off-Off Broadway, then a long-running hit Off Broadway, for which he received the New York Drama Critics Circle Award. (Indeed, *Hot L Baltimore* is so conventional that it has provided the basis, or at least the title, for a TV situation comedy—though Wilson doubtless was surprised to find he had written a comedy.)

Lady Bright is one of almost two dozen plays by Wilson produced off-Off Broadway. *This Is the Rill Speaking* (1966) and *The Rimers of Eldritch* (1966) are among the best and best-known. More recently, he has had two works produced commercially, *The Gingham Dog* on Broadway in 1969, for a short run, and *Lemon Sky* in 1970, also for a short run.

Leslie Bright is about forty, 'a screaming preening queen, rapidly losing a long-kept "beauty".' On a hot afternoon in summer, he has returned to his one-room apartment, whose walls are adorned with hundreds of signatures, most prominent among them 'Adam' and 'Michael Delaney'. The only other characters are a boy and girl, who embody various lovers, moods and memories from Leslie's past. And, for Leslie, all now does seem to *be* past. As he remembers former lovers, seeks unsuccessfully to raise one of them on the phone, stares at his aging reflection in the mirror, he is a picture of approaching madness. The play is virtually a monologue, a poignant testimony to the truth of the Boy's statement, 'It's a terrible thing to wake up to loneliness'. It is at times flamboyant, almost always touching, a work possessing a very rare combination of compassion and wit.

The title for *The Gingham Dog* comes from Eugene Field's late-nineteenth century work 'The Duel': 'The gingham dog went bow-wow-wow! And the calico cat replied mee-ow! The air was littered, an hour or so, with bits of gingham and calico.'

The Gingham Dog examines inter-racial marriage, its frequent tensions and frustrations and, by extension, its reflection of overall relations between black and white in America. As it opens, the marriage between Gloria and Vincent is in the process of breaking up after three years, the first of them happy and rewarding, the remaining two a slow process of disintegration of their love and ability to communicate with each other.

As they pack cartons preparatory to Vincent's departure, they unfold the emotions, patterns and events that have contributed to the dissolution of their marriage, among them the fact that Gloria has become what Vincent calls a 'professional Negro', and Vincent compromised his aspirations by taking a job in a mid-town architectural firm. As they alternately muse and shout their vituperation, they are joined briefly by Robert, an effeminate neighbour, and Barbara, Vincent's very Southern sister, who sets out to display how 'liberal' she is but winds up showing quite the opposite

By the end of the first act, which has some very funny moments and some shafts of truth that strike very near the core of the couple's—and perhaps the country's—dilemma, Wilson has said just about all he has to say (and could easily have said all of it). Instead, Vincent returns early the following morning for a long, often arid rehash of 'why' it's all happened, only briefly redeemed by some wistful reflections on whether we should all perhaps be hoping for some 'little green people' from outer space on whom we could unite to vent our hate, our frustration and our fear.

In *Lemon Sky*, Wilson tells of how seventeen-year-old Alan journeys to his father's home in California, a father he has not seen since he was a child. What he has undertaken is part confrontation, part voyage of self-discovery. He and Douglas have, of course, nothing to talk about—or, if they do, it will be avoided. The father has remarried and has two young sons. Their ranch-style home also shelters two girls, wards of the state, one a self-proclaimed nymphomaniac, the other a younger, more studious type.

Although Alan is welcomed with open arms, those arms, at least where his father is concerned, soon close. His arrival throws the tenuous and peculiar personality mix out of balance, setting up a series of confrontations—and Wilson can be very good with the set-piece confrontation—but also slipping at times perilously close to soap opera.

Lemon Sky's attenuated, essentially slice-of-life scenes never really achieve much momentum and its insights seldom delve below a too apparent surface, with the result that not even a wealth of superbly playable dialogue can rescue it.

As noted, *The Hot L Baltimore* won the 1973 New York Drama Critics Circle Award as the best play of the season and went on to run for well over two years Off Broadway. It takes place in the once elegant, now decaying Hotel Baltimore, earlier the site of gracious living, now only a flophouse, a haven for whores and the cast-offs of society. In days gone by, it had been one of many hotels located near a railroad terminal. And, 'its history has mirrored the [American] rails' decline'. In

1973, it is about to be demolished; even the sign outside, with its missing 'e', reflects the times it has come upon.

Through the lounge pass three whores, principal among them The Girl, nineteen and filled with a romantic enthusiasm for the railroads of the old days, excited about almost anything (which perhaps is a help in her trade) and eager to assist young Paul Granger III, who has come in search of his missing grandfather. Through it also pass Jackie, a young woman of twenty-four, pretty and vulnerable despite the fact that she effects a 'manner, voice and stance [that] are those of a young stevedore', a natural food freak, and her younger brother, Jamie, who are on their way to Utah to the twenty acres of land Jackie has acquired, where they want to raise their own crops. 'We don't need no house. We're sleeping in a sleeping bag.'

The Girl has passed through the area on one of her train rides. She knows it is a wasteland, that Jackie has been duped, that their dreams are doomed to frustration. As, apparently, are the dreams and lives of virtually all those in the Hotel Baltimore. Its time may be coming to an end in thirty days, its years of glory come only to decay and destruction. Its residents, transient and permanent, seem fated for nothing more.

Hot L Baltimore is a sad and funny play. If its insights are generally less than profound and its characters at times little more than clichés, it nonetheless is *real*, in touch with life rather than abstractions, absorbed with American roots in a way that only one or two other playwrights of Wilson's generation are, Sam Shepard being the most obvious, though he writes in an altogether different style.

Coming immediately after *Hot L Baltimore*, *The Mound Builders* (1975) was a considerable disappointment, not to mention a considerable bore. A group of people have come together on the site of an archaeological dig in Southern Illinois. They include Dr August Howe, the senior archaeologist, and his wife and daughter, a younger archaeologist and his pregnant wife and the novelist sister of the older man, an alcoholic trying to dry out after a lengthy period of 'living in a liquid world'. They are periodically joined by an outsider, Chad Jasker, the son of the owner of the property on which they are conducting their dig for artifacts of the ancient 'mound builders', Indians who inhabited the region perhaps a thousand years ago.

Seemingly, such a situation would contain ample opportunities to explore each character's nature and attitudes, their approaches to life and their ideas concerning Man's destiny. Seemingly, it would also offer the occasion for major conflicts and confrontations among this diverse group of people. Sadly, it does not, for they are not people but insufficiently explored, inadequately motivated puppets in the playwright's hands. Only the sister and, fleetingly, the young man intent upon turning the property, his property, into a lucrative site of highways, dams and motels, thus obliterating forever the lost civilization, come alive. Only at the end, does the conflict between two approaches to civilization—and life—come into focus. Before that, there is endless rumination, endless padding, endless pseudo-profundity. The senior archaeologist shows his slides and ventures his generally cynical or sardonic comments; the younger characters bicker and muse and get drunk, but never become individuals.

In *Hot L Baltimore*, the decline of the once illustrious hotel became a strikingly effective metaphor for the decline and disillusion of dreams of the inhabitants. The 'mound builders' metaphor never becomes an even remotely effective one. Men—the archaeologists—may seek to build their own scholarly monuments and others—the young Chad—theirs in the form of motels and fortunes, but a play must have more life, more living figures, to make such a metaphor resonant and dramatically viable. It must reach considerably farther beneath the surface, not settle for the superficial characterization and amateur psychology of *The Mound Builders* if it is to have anything truly worth saying about ourselves or our past.

Jason Miller has had only one play produced thus far, *That Championship Season* (1972), and, with his recent success as a film actor in *The Exorcist* and elsewhere it remains to be seen when he will continue to write, at least other than sporadically, for the theatre. Yet, that one play, which received virtually all the 'best play' awards of the season in America, is very much worthy of attention despite its London failure. One of the reasons it is, is its highly American character, its reflection of American myths and rituals. For Americans over twenty-five or thirty—and perhaps those under it—it has tremendous resonance and, without belabouring it with excessive intellectual trappings, a considerable amount to say about the way we live.

In America at least, though surely elsewhere as well, the language of sports has become the language of politics and foreign policy. Perhaps it is a subconscious nostalgia for the day when clear-cut 'victory' was possible, when there was a definite and well-defined 'enemy' and the objective, to 'win', was not merely honourable but attainable. Players didn't go on strike any more than students protested. The guy who led the league was a hero—and so was the flier who led the air-strike. Everybody loved a winner. (In fact, as we all know, everybody still does; it's only that we've become a bit shy about admitting it.) Only in sports is it still occasionally respectable and, even there, if one is reflective, one has to wonder.

That Championship Season takes place in the living room of the coach's house in a small town somewhere in the Lackawanna Valley of Pennsylvania. It is that rarity these days: a play, a melodrama if one is to be honest, with a beginning, a middle and an end. It has characters to 'identify' with and emotions that are clear and relatively uncomplicated.

Two decades before, Fillmore High School came from behind in the last ten seconds to become the 1952 Pennsylvania State Champions. Now, four of the starting five are meeting to celebrate the anniversary, meeting to reminisce over the moment that remains the high point of their lives. The fifth is mysteriously missing. The trophy they won stands on a table near the window; a scratchy phonograph record recalls their unforgettable ten seconds, the ten seconds that cause the former coach to remind them: 'You were a legend in your times, boys.'

'What happened?' asks one of them, for a moment voicing the doubt, the disenchantment, the failed dreams, that hide behind the early boisterous camaraderie and alcohol. What happened indeed? George is the mayor, running for re-election and an apparent sure loser in his campaign against a Jew who has committed the further indiscretion of being 'an ecology nut'. James is a junior high school principal, a colourless and frustrated man whose sole hope for advancement lies with the mayor. He feels himself being swallowed up by anonymity and, he says, 'I want my share.' His brother, Tom, the play's Cassandra, is also the play's drunk. The author's mouthpiece, he alone speaks the truth for any sustained moment. Phil, the last of the quartet, is a wealthy businessman, ready to abandon financing George's campaign because George looks like being a loser. Phil, a cut-throat strip-mine man, only plays winners.

The coach senses dissension in the room and he is unwilling to let his 'team' fall apart. 'Dissension is destroying this country.' They must all pull together; they must *win*, even if winning means breaking the rules; even if it means George must ignore Phil's affair with his wife; even if it means James must sacrifice his role as campaign manager. 'Exploiting a man's weakness is the name of the game', part of the American ethic. The other name of the game is *winning*. As the football coach Vince Lombardi once said, it 'isn't everything—it's the only thing'.

The seeds of the dissension are, however, in the past, specifically in that championship season and in the society that contributed to it. How, after all, did they win in the first place? Why is it that Martin, the star of their triumph, is absent? Why? Because the coach, on that memorable night, told him to 'get that nigger center, the kangaroo', and he broke the boy's ribs. The truth, Tom tells the coach, is that they 'stole the trophy'. The truth, says the coach, is that 'We won. That trophy is the truth, the only truth'.

The coach's 'boys', his 'real trophy', are a microcosm of a declining, increasingly purposeless America. They are empty and self-important, insecure and ambitious, venally motivated and capable of almost any treachery or duplicity. And they would seem to know not what they do. 'We are the country, boys', says the coach.

A little of such lines clearly goes a long way and fortunately Miller for the most part stops short of hammering home his moral and provides some funny, indeed very funny, dialogue. With *That Championship Season* he perfectly catches the atmosphere, the attitudes and the moral ambivalence of a large segment of the population, that part which does not recognize that what Tom says of the team is for many in the world equally true of the image of the nation in which he says it: 'We're a myth.' It will come as no surprise at all *That Championship Season* does not have a happy ending.

Arthur Kopit has thus far belied the early promise of the
bizarre *Oh Dad, Poor Dad, Mamma's Hung You in the Closet
and I'm Feelin' So Sad* (1960). Only with *Indians* (1969),
produced by the Royal Shakespeare Company in
London prior to its New York production, has he approached it.

In its New York production at least, *Indians* was what
might be termed neo-Brechtian (much more so than in
London). It offfers what is, in effect, a dual framework,
on the one hand the investigation of Indian grievances
by a presidential commission at the Standing Rock
reservation, on the other Buffalo Bill's Wild West Show.
Within this, Kopit juxtaposes the Indians' dignity with
the white man's farce, the glory that was the former's
heritage and the hypocrisy that is the latter's. If he
makes it all too black and white, too much a re-run in
reverse of the day when cowboys were automatically the
good guys and Indians bloodthirsty savages, he also for
the most part avoids the sort of sentimentality his
material might have led to.

Amid stereophonic tom-toms and circus noises, if the
author's script is to be serviced, Buffalo Bill Cody comes
galloping on astride a 'horse'. With lights flashing about
him and loudspeakers to remind him to get on with the
show as he attempts to elicit the audience's sympathy, he
is launched into an alternating series of sequences. They
recall his slaughter of 4280 buffalo to provide food for
the railroad workers going west and the resultant
hunger of the Indians, the subsequent duplicity of
Washington as it reneged on Jefferson's pledge that 'not
a foot of land will be taken from the Indians without
their consent' and upon various treaties.

If there is a bit too much of the stereotyped noble
savage about Mr Kopit's Indians, they are moving
nonetheless, especially when given their own words, as
with Chief Joseph's speech of surrender, which he is
reduced to repeating before Buffalo Bill's Wild West
Show audiences: 'My heart is sick and sad. From where
the sun now stands, I will fight no more forever.'

Through it all, Buffalo Bill himself wanders, bemused, blustering, justifying, only half understanding
the role he has played for both white men and Indians.
'I had a dream', he says, 'that I was gonna help people,
great numbers of people.' He is the ineffectual, well-
intentioned man with his heart at least partly in the right
place, the man whose error is that he knows not what he

does, save perhaps at the moment when, the government's partial genocide of the Indians completed, he comes forward to peddle his phony souvenirs of the civilization that was, pleading, 'Anybody who thinks we have done something wrong is wrong'.

Indians remains a play more successful in some of its moments than it eventually is in its totality, with a structure and a development that are too erratic to be fully satisfying. Fragmented and powerful, dazzling and annoying, it is a work in the realm of the might-have-been, one whose realization on stage has yet to achieve the potential of its idea or the fulfilment of its aspiration. If that can be said of any drama that does not fully 'work', it remains perhaps more true of *Indians* than of most.

One always hopes for a writer such as Kopit, a writer of imagination, a writer who dares. But the years do pass, the plays do not come, and it becomes ever harder to think of him as in any sense a 'major' writer of the period since World War II.

For the most part, even the better-known of the younger generation of American playwrights—by now, in fact, the middle generation—have accomplished relatively little of continuing interest. Israel Horovitz, Paul Foster, Leonard Melfi, Tom Eyen, Rochelle Owens, Megan Terry, Rosalyn Drexler, Maria Irene Fornes, even Terrence McNally, who seems to have gone over to the Establishment, and others have generally failed to move on from where they began. Or at least much beyond it. Michael Weller may be an exception, or may in the future prove to be, but most of his work has been staged not in America but in London and I have elected not to discuss it here. In *Cancer* (in America called *Moonchildren*), he displayed a not inconsiderable talent, though he did not in reality write a genuinely effective play. He has recently returned to the United States and become associated with Joseph Papp's New York Shakespeare Festival, but it remains to be seen what will evolve. He is, perhaps, the best hope for the future, since he combines both technique and a certain degree of insight, without the self-indulgence of most of his contemporaries.

This book has not discussed America's black playwrights, though I have written extensively concerning them in the past both for British and American publications. LeRoi Jones is surely one of the three or four best playwrights of his generation, though he has in recent years turned his attention from the theatre to politics and it has been several years since he has written a play. Ed Bullins prefers to write for black audiences, though his work has been produced elsewhere. He is a writer of enormous power and resonance. Charles Gordone, Douglas Turner Ward and Adrienne Kennedy began well, but have not, in recent years, come up with plays that measured up to their earliest work. (Gordone, in fact, has yet to write a follow-up to his first, 1969, play, the stunning *No Place to Be Somebody*.) Almost without exception, they prefer to be reviewed by black critics, though, of necessity, submitting to the 'white' criticism of the daily and periodical press. Although I do not share their outlook, regarding a play as a play regardless of its national, racial or ethnic origins, I have elected to honour this preference.

10 Conclusion

In the introduction, I quoted two statements by Paddy Chayefsky, the first made in 1969, after the disappointment of *The Latent Heterosexual* failing to make it to Broadway: 'Broadway as a legitimate theatre is moribund'; the second in 1975, after a series of film successes: 'In the foreseeable future, I see nothing for me on Broadway. The theatre has become a kind of unnecessary institution.'

In general, there is little to take exception to in the first and equally little in the first portion of the second. The serious American playwright of today has almost no possibility of 'making it' on Broadway. He has, in fact, scant possibility of making it *to* Broadway. Occasionally, a 'serious' British play does—generally one that had its first exposure at one of London's institutional theatres and arrives with the aura of international success—but even they are rarities and this is not the place to explore whether an *Equus* or a *Hadrian VII* would have enjoyed a comparably long run had they arrived in New York 'cold', without an advance ticket sale and the London cachet that still carries inordinate weight—inordinate, that is, in the same sense that the idea of a Broadway hit musical still carries disproportionate weight outside New York.

The first thing that should be acknowledged is that this is a situation that is not going to improve at any time in the foreseeable future, if ever. The American playwright who is looking to Broadway is not suddenly going to find David Merrick, Alexander Cohen, Harold Prince or Roger Stevens eagerly awaiting him, option cheque in hand, at Forty-fourth or Forty-fifth and Broadway. The Messrs Merrick, Cohen, Prince and Stevens are far more likely to be found on Shaftesbury Avenue or at the National or Aldwych. Unless they are doing musicals or an occasional comedy by a proven box office draw, they want pre-tested products.

Some of the 'products' are, of course, being pre-tested in America's regional theatres, though hardly as many as the ballyhoo over the rare resulting production in or transfer to New York would indicate. Regional theatre in America as elsewhere is essentially a tributary theatre, one that keeps its doors open primarily because of the hits that flow in from New York not the hits it sends there. A certain few regional theatres are offering distinguished 'premieres', but for the most part they are 'American premieres' of other than American plays. One can only laud this on the non-chauvinistic level, but it offers only minor comfort to the American playwright.

When the New York Shakespeare Festival took up residence at Lincoln Center in 1973, producer Joseph Papp proclaimed a 'new American play' policy, in contrast with the previous producer's series of revivals, in the larger of the two theatres. Shakespeare was to be presented in the smaller one, which may or may not have been a well-thought-out decision. In the event, the first two seasons of Shakespeare unveiled a series of productions that too often seemed to be staged simply for the sake of staging them, rather than out of any producer's or director's commitment to the plays. On the other hand, the much larger Vivian Beaumont Theatre, which with its thrust stage would have been ideal for Shakespeare, was instead the scene for the new-play policy and far more often than not it proved precisely the wrong location for the works being presented, beginning with the very first of them, David Rabe's *In the Boom Boom Room*, subsequently produced far more effectively though still not successfully at the smaller Public Theatre.

Although one could, and I am sure Mr Papp would, make a case for the New York Shakespeare Festival leading its audiences from Shakespeare and Molière and Gorky and Brecht to Rabe and Miguel Pinero and Anne Burr and Bill Gunn, not to mention introducing new audiences to Lincoln Center, the playwrights themselves, or at least the works in question, were not at a stage to stand up under either the Lincoln Center limelight or the overproduction they received.

The reason for raising this, however, has nothing to do with the success or failure of the plays in question, but rather with why, if the New York Shakespeare Festival's mainstage, rather than its more appropriate smaller theatre, was to be used for new plays, they had to be exclusively the plays of writers who, in most instances, simply are not yet ready for this degree of exposure. One can make something of a fetish of introducing and continuing to produce even the poor work of 'new American writers', as the NYSF has, while at the same time failing to recognize that 'new' and 'good' are not necessarily or even frequently synonymous. Might not the more recent plays of Williams, Miller, Albee and, for that matter, others who have simply given up on the commercial theatre, have fared better within the more sympathetic environs of the New York Shakespeare Festival? They surely would have had longer runs, given the Lincoln Center subscription audience. With all due respect to Mr Papp's commitment to *young* writers, a commitment that has provided the major creative force in the American theatre in recent years, there should be no automatic codicil that excludes their elders. After two seasons of generally poorly received new plays, the NYSF reverted to the classics and brought in 'stars' at Lincoln Center in the Autumn of 1975. With customary adventurousness, Papp simultaneously launched a new American playwrights series on Broadway.

In the American theatre of today, the playwright seemingly must be one of three things: young (which seemingly means, very), a 'classic' (which means that his early plays may receive respectful revivals, e.g., Tennessee Williams, but his later ones often fall by the wayside) or Neil Simon (which means he may decide to move to Hollywood). There is no acceptable reason for this, for it makes no sense at all that proven playwrights, even though they may not be 'great' talents, should have to abandon playwriting in favour of more lucrative forms, while untalented amateurs and semi-professionals are the beneficiaries of major Government and Foundation grants and production by similarly endowed companies over a period of years without producing any work of consequence. Yet, this is precisely what is happening and certainly one of the primary reasons for the failure of development in any number of writers who could be making a valuable contribution to the theatre.

In the introduction, though seldom elsewhere, I have suggested that there are bright spots. And, having commented negatively on the plays and policy the New York Shakespeare Festival pursued at Lincoln Center, it is obligatory to say that the same company's approach to productions at its Off Broadway Public Theatre has been almost totally admirable. It displays the Festival's what, where and why—its reason for being—in terms of the contemporary theatre, and, if one needed any further indication of that it was provided by the fact that, almost precisely a year after Rabe's *Boom Boom Room* was almost universally decried at Lincoln Center, even to the point of having the producer's and the playwright's motivations called into question by the critic for the *New York Times*, the same producer had the loyalty to his playwright—not to mention the facilities—to give a revised version of the play a second hearing. It is unfortunate that William Inge, with *A Loss of Roses*, Williams with more than one of his plays and doubtless any number of others were not, and are not being offered a similar opportunity. Without it, it is difficult to hold out much hope for playwrights who do not happen to strike Mr Papp's fancy, though, as it happens, some of them are among the most talented in the current American theatre.

There are any number of good or potentially good American playwrights on hand today. They range from their twenties to their forties and beyond. A few of them are potentially better than good, whatever the ultimate fate of their reputations. Yet, they are neither achieving their potential nor attracting any substantial audience. Their plays are opening on Tuesday or Wednesday and closing on the following Saturday all too many times a season or else playing a dozen or so 'showcase' performances off-Off Broadway, seldom if ever to be seen again. No one would suggest that this is unique to America. For what once was an adventurous country, however, America has rarely provided a very adventurous theatre audience. It would be pleasant every so often to think that the majority won't always rule, at least in the arts. Or perhaps merely to figure out why it does, which is probably a far more important question if the theatre is again to play a major role either as entertainment or as an influence. The playwrights themselves are there.

Playlist

Edward Albee

All Over, Atheneum, New York 1971; Cape, London 1972

The American Dream, Coward-McCann, New York 1961

A Delicate Balance, Atheneum, New York 1966; Cape, London 1968

Seascape, Atheneum, New York 1975

Tiny Alice, Atheneum, New York 1965; Cape, London, 1966

Who's Afraid of Virginia Woolf?, Atheneum, New York 1962; Penguin Books 1972

The Zoo Story, *The Death of Bessie Smith* and *The Sandbox*, Coward-McCann, New York 1960

William Inge

Bus Stop, Random House, New York 1955; English Theatre Guild, London

Come Back, Little Sheba, Random House, New York 1950

The Dark at the Top of the Stairs, Random House, New York, 1958; English Theatre Guild, London

A Loss of Roses, Random House, New York 1960

Picnic, Random House, New York 1953; English Theatre Guild, London

Arthur Kopit

Indians, Hill and Wang, New York 1969; Eyre Methuen, London 1970

Oh Dad, Poor Dad, Mamma's Hung You in the Closet and I'm Feelin' So Sad, Hill and Wang, New York 1960

Arthur Miller

After the Fall, Viking, New York 1968

All My Sons (in *Collected Plays*), Viking, New York 1957, Heinemann, London 1971

The Creation of the World and Other Business, Viking, New York 1973

The Crucible, Viking, New York 1953; Penguin Books, London 1970

Death of a Salesman (in *Collected Plays*), Viking, New York 1957; Heinemann, London 1968

Incident at Vichy, Viking, New York 1965; English Theatre Guild, London

The Price, Viking, New York 1968; Penguin Books, London 1970

A View from the Bridge, Viking, New York 1955; Penguin Books, London 1969

Jason Miller

That Championship Season, Atheneum, New York 1972

Eugene O'Neill

All God's Chillun Got Wings, Boni and Liveright, New York 1924; Cape, London 1973

Days without End, Random House, New York 1934

Desire Under the Elms, Boni and Liveright, New York 1925

The Hairy Ape, Boni and Liveright, New York 1921; Cape, London 1973

The Iceman Cometh, Random House, New York 1946; Cape, London 1966

Long Day's Journey into Night, Yale University Press, New Haven, Connecticut, 1956; Cape, London 1966

(Note: O'Neill's plays are available in numerous editions. Those above are primarily the original publications; all have been reissued in more recent editions, primarily by Random House.)

David Rabe

The Basic Training of Pavlo Hummel and Sticks and Bones, Viking, New York 1973

In the Boom Boom Room, Knopf, New York 1975

Sam Shepard

Five Plays by Sam Shepard (includes *Fourteen Hundred Thousand, Red Cross, Chicago, Icarus's Mother* and *Melodrama Play*), Bobbs-Merrill, New York 1967; Faber, London 1969

La Turista, Bobbs-Merrill, New York 1968

Mad Dog Blues and Other Plays (includes *Cowboy Mouth*, *The Rock Garden*, *Cowboys* 2) Winter House, New York 1972

Operation Sidewinder, Bobbs-Merrill, New York 1970

The Tooth of Crime and *Geography of a Horse Dreamer*, Grove Press, New York 1974

The Unseen Hand and Other Plays (includes *Forensic and the Navigators*, *The Holy Ghostly*, *Back Bog Beast Bait*, *Shaved Splits*, *4-H Club*), Bobbs-Merrill, New York 1972

Neil Simon

Barefoot in the Park, Random House, New York 1964

The Comedy of Neil Simon (collected plays), Random House, New York 1973

The Gingerbread Lady, Random House, New York 1971

God's Favorite, Random House, New York 1975

The Good Doctor, Random House, New York 1974

Last of the Red Hot Lovers, Random House, New York 1970

The Odd Couple, Random House, New York 1966

Plaza Suite, Random House, New York 1969

The Prisoner of Second Avenue, Random House, New York 1972

The Star-Spangled Girl, Random House, New York 1967

The Sunshine Boys, Random House, New York 1973

Jean-Claude van Itallie

America Hurrah (includes *Interview*, *TV* and *Motel*), Coward-McCann, New York 1967; English Theatre Guild, London

The Serpent, Atheneum, New York 1969

Tennessee Williams

Camino Real, New Directions, New York 1953; Secker and Warburg, London 1958

Cat on a Hot Tin Roof (revised version), New Directions, New York, 1975; English Theatre Guild, London

Dragon Country (includes *In the Bar of a Tokyo Hotel*, *Confessional* and six other plays), New Directions, New York 1970

The Glass Menagerie, New Directions, New York 1945; Heinemann, London 1968

The Milk Train Doesn't Stop Here Anymore, New Directions, New York 1964; English Theatre Guild, London

The Night of the Iguana, New Directions, New York 1963; Secker and Warburg, London 1963

Orpheus Descending, New Directions, New York 1958; English Theatre Guild, London

Out Cry, New Directions, New York 1973

Period of Adjustment, New Directions, New York 1960; Secker and Warburg, London 1961

The Rose Tattoo, New Directions, New York 1951; Penguin Books, London 1968

Small Craft Warnings, New Directions, New York 1972

A Streetcar Named Desire, New Directions, New York 1947

Suddenly Last Summer, New Directions, New York 1958; English Theatre Guild, London

Sweet Bird of Youth, New Directions, New York 1959; Penguin Books, London 1969

Lanford Wilson

The Gingham Dog, Hill and Wang, New York, 1969; English Theatre Guild, London

The Hot L Baltimore, Hill and Wang, New York 1973

The Rimers of Eldritch and Other Plays (including *Days Ahead*, *The Madness of Lady Bright*, *This Is the Rill Speaking* and *Wandering*), Hill and Wang, New York 1967; English Theatre Guild, London

Index